ANNE FRANK IN THE WORLD

D1717266

DIE WELT DER ANNE FRANK

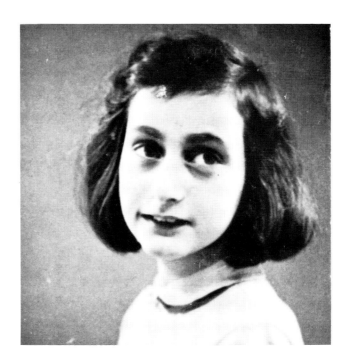

ANNE FRANK STICHTING

1929 — **1945**

IE WELT DER **ANNE FRANK**

4

© text: Anne Frank Stichting, Amsterdam
© illustrations: see list of illustrations
ISBN 90-72972-09-0

first edition June 1985
second edition December 1985
third, revised edition December 1989
fourth, revised edition January 1992
fifth, revised edition January 1993

Text: Anne Frank Stiftung, Amsterdam.
© Illustrationen: siehe Liste der Illustrationen

Erste Ausgabe Juni 1985
Zweite Ausgabe Oktober 1988
Dritte Ausgabe August 1991
Vierte Ausgabe Januar 1993

PREFACE

Had Anne Frank – an ordinary young Jewish girl – lived next door, could she have counted on us for help during the Nazi occupation? This is the question this exhibit forces us to ask, again and again.

Before the Nazis came to power Germany was afflicted by rampant poverty and unemployment. Hitler, exploiting widespread anti-Semitic prejudice, blamed 'the Jews', making them into the scapegoats for the country's problems.

Hitler announced openly and quite frankly that he intended to abolish democracy and to deprive 'non-Aryans', like the Jews, of their civil rights. In spite of this, one-third of the German population voted for Hitler's Nazi party, the NSDAP. As a result of these elections, the Nazi party, as the largest single party, was entitled to form the government.

In this way millions of ordinary citizens brought Hitler to power. When subsequently, as Hitler had announced, democracy was indeed abolished and the persecution of political opponents and Jews commenced, resistance immediately became difficult.

Few people became active in the resistance. The majority remained indifferent. In the countries occupied by the Nazis, including the Netherlands, the situation was much the same.

The ideas of National Socialism, carried out to the extremes, caused the death of millions of people. Nevertheless, these cruel ideas still exist throughout the world.

Even today, people still look for a scapegoat to blame for their troubles. Anti-Semitic and other racist prejudice lives on, building barriers between people and creating discrimination.

The Anne Frank Center hopes to convince visitors that resistance against discrimination is necessary from the start. Had this conviction shaped the consciousness of the voters in 1932, then the name Adolf Hitler would be totally insignificant to us today.

VORWORT

Hätte Anne Frank, zu Lebzeiten ein Mädchen unter vielen, auf unsere Hilfe rechnen können, wäre sie unser Nachbarskind gewesen?

Bevor Hitler an die Macht kam, herrschten in Deutschland Arbeitslosigkeit und Armut. Hitler nutzte weit verbreitete antise-mitische Vorurteile aus. Er schob den Juden die Schuld in die Schuhe und machte sie zum Sündenbock für alle Mißstände.

Hitler kündigte unmißverständlich an, daß er die Demokratie abschaffen und die Juden entrechten würde. Trotzdem stimmten 1932 mehr als 13 Mio. Menschen für Hitlers NSDAP. Ihre Stimmen brachten Hitler an die Macht. In der Hoffnung, sich selber von allen Problemen zu befreien, ließen sie die Juden fallen.

Als die Demokratie, wie angekündigt, aufgelöst wurde und die Verfolgung politischer Gegner und der Juden begann, war Wider-stand plötzlich erheblich schwieriger. Nur wenige zeigten sich solidarisch mit den Verfolgten und leisteten Widerstand. Die überwältigende Mehrheit ließ sich begeistern oder verhielt sich gleichgültig.

Die Ideen des Nationalsozialismus haben in ihrer äußersten Konsequenz Millionen Menschen das Leben gekostet.
Trotzdem leben viele dieser Ideen weiter.
Immer noch suchen viele von uns einen Sündenbock, eine Gruppe, die Schuld ist an allen Problemen.
Noch immer leben wir mit antisemitischen und rassistischen Vorurteilen, die Keile zwischen Menschen treiben und Diskrimi-nierung möglich machen.

Die Anne Frank Stiftung hofft, mit dieser Ausstellung deutlich zu machen, daß Widerstand gegen Diskriminierung bei den ersten Anzeichen beginnen muß.
Hätten die Wähler dies 1932 erkannt, würde uns der Name Adolf Hitler heute nichts mehr sagen.

TABLE OF CONTENTS

INHALT

10

Ancestors of Anne Frank have lived in Frankfurt since the 17th century. Otto Frank, Anne's father, is born on May 12, 1889, on Frankfurt's Westend (West side), a well-to-do neighborhood. His father is a banker. Otto Frank attends high school and briefly studies art at the University of Heidelberg. Via a friend he is offered and accepts a job from 1908 until 1909 at Macy's Department Store in New York. When his father dies, Otto Frank returns to Germany and works for a metal engineering company in Düsseldorf until 1914. During World War I he and his two brothers serve in the German Army, where Otto attains the rank of lieutenant. After the war he works in his father's bank, but banks are not faring well at that time. While at the bank he becomes acquainted with Edith Holländer, the daughter of a manufacturer. Born in 1900, she grows up in Aachen. Otto and Edith marry in 1925 and settle in Frankfurt. They have two daughters, Margot, born in 1926, and Anne, whose full name is Annelies Marie, born on June 12, 1929.

Die Vorfahren Anne Franks lebten seit dem 17. Jahrhundert in Frankfurt. Annes Vater Otto Frank (1889) wächst im reichen Stadtteil Westend als Sohn eines Bankiers auf. Nach dem Abitur studiert er kurze Zeit Kunst in Heidelberg. Die Jahre 1908/09 verbringt er in den USA, wo er durch Vermittlung eines Freundes beim großen Warenhauskonzern 'Macy' arbeiten kann. Als sein Vater im Sterben liegt, kehrt er nach Deutschland zurück. Bis 1914 arbeitet Otto Frank in einem metallverarbeitenden Betrieb in Düsseldorf. Im 1. Weltkrieg dient er im Deutschen Heer und wird zum Leutnant befördert. Nach dem Krieg tritt er der Bank seines Vaters bei.

In jenen Jahren lernt Otto Frank Edith Holländer aus Aachen kennen. 1925 heiraten die beiden und beschließen in Frankfurt zu wohnen. 1926 wird Margot geboren, und drei Jahre später folgt Annelies Marie, genannt Anne.

1 Family portrait, circa 1900. Front row, Otto Frank in navy suit.
2 Brothers Herbert, left, and Otto Frank in the German army, 1916.
3 Edith Holländer.
4 Edith Holländer and Otto Frank during their honeymoon in San Remo, 1925.

1 Die Familie Frank in Wildbad. In der ersten Reihe im Matrosenanzug, Otto Frank. Um 1900.
2 Otto Frank (rechts) mit seinem Bruder Herbert in Uniform. Um 1916.
3 Edith Holländer.
4 Hochzeitsreise nach San Remo, 1925.

Otto Frank is an enthusiastic amateur photographer. He takes dozens of photographs of Anne and Margot playing in the street with their friends, visiting their grandparents in Aachen, or going to the countryside.

Otto Frank ist ein begeisterter Hobbyfotograf. Von Anne und Margot hat er viele Fotos gemacht, zu Hause, auf der Straße, mit Freundinnen, bei Kinderfesten, bei den Großeltern in Aachen und so weiter.

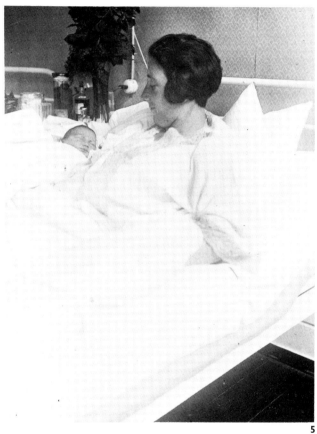

5

5 Anne Frank, one day old, with her mother. June 13, 1929.
6 Margot with her new sister, July, 1929.
7 Margot and Anne.
8 Anne with her mother in Ganghoferstrasse, 1931.

5 Anne Frank, am Tage nach der Geburt mit ihrer Mutter, 13. Juni 1929.
6 Margot mit dem neuen Schwesterchen, Juli 1929.
7 Margot und Anne.
8 Anne mit ihrer Mutter in der Ganghoferstraße, 1931.

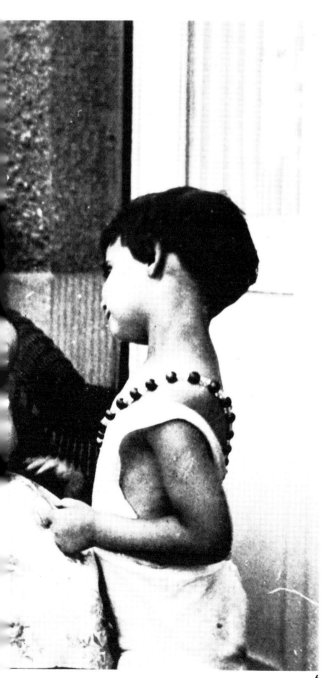

6

7

8

14

9 *Anne.*
10 *Otto, Anne and Margot Frank, 1931.*
11 *Anne and Margot.*
12 *Edith Frank with her two daughters near the Hauptwache in Frankfurt's city center, 1933.*
13 *Anne, 1932.*

9 *Anne.*
10 *Otto Frank mit seinen Töchtern, 1931.*
11 *Anne und Margot.*
12 *Edith Frank mit ihren Töchtern bei der Hauptwache im Frankfurter Zentrum. 1933.*
13 *Anne, 1932.*

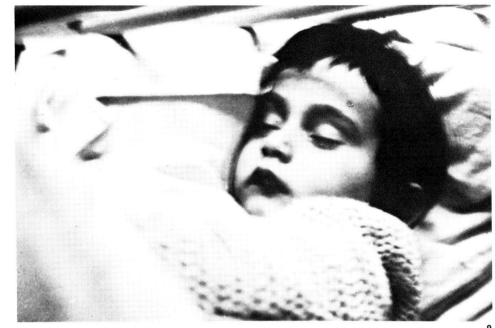

9

10

11

12

13

6 FRANKFURT AM MAIN IN THE 1920S – PORTRAIT OF A CITY

6 FRANKFURT AM MAIN IN DEN 20ER JAHREN – BILD EINER STADT

Since the Middle Ages Frankfurt has been an important center of trade and finance. At the end of the 19th century new industrial areas spring up on the east and west side of the city. After annexing surrounding villages, Frankfurt has the largest land area of all German cities at the end of World War I. In 1929 the city has a population of 540,000. Tradition and modernization go hand in hand, and as a result, Frankfurt is an attractive, modern city economically, socially and culturally. The intellectual and political climate is democratic and liberal. The city is governed by a coalition of the social democratic, liberal and christian parties.

Seit dem Mittelalter ist Frankfurt ein wichtiges Handelszentrum in Deutschland. Ende des 19. Jahrhunderts entstehen am Rande der Stadt große Industriegebiete. Nach dem 1. Weltkrieg ist Frankfurt zeitweise die flächenmäßig größte Stadt Deutschlands. 1929 leben hier 540.000 Menschen. Das geistig-politische Klima ist demokratisch und progressiv.

14 Panoramic view of Frankfurt am Main. At left, the Dome, where the German kings and emperors were crowned until 1806. Photo circa 1932.
15 Parts of the inner city in decay, 1924.
16 The new living quarters offer modern schools, playgrounds and various facilities. Circa 1930.

14 Ansicht der Frankfurter Altstadt von Süden mit dem Dom, bis 1806 Krönungsort der deutschen Kaiser und Könige. Um 1932.
15 Die Schattenseite der Frankfurter Altstadt: Slums und Elendsquartiere, 1924.
16 Die neuen Siedlungen erhielten moderne Schulbauten, Sozialeinrichtungen und Kinderspiel-plätze. Um 1930.

15

16

14

7 FRANKFURT, 1929 – POLITICAL AND ECONOMIC CRISIS

7 FRANKFURT AM MAIN UM 1929 – KRISE VON DEMOKRATIE UND ÖKONOMIE

The Great Depression of 1929 causes social and political tension in Frankfurt. Between 1929 and 1932 industrial activity decreases 65%. By the end of 1932, more than 70,000 people are unemployed in Frankfurt. One-fourth of the population – workers and civil servants, in particular – no longer has a steady income. Furthermore, the National Socialists profit from the inability of the democratic system to solve the crisis. The labor movement carries the weight in the political struggle against the threat from the extreme right.

1929: Im Geburtsjahr Anne Franks bricht die Weltwirtschaftskrise aus. Überall verschärfen sich soziale und politische Gegensätze. Zwischen 1929 und 1932 schrumpft die industrielle Produktion in Frankfurt um 65%. Ende 1932 gibt es über 70.000 Arbeitslose. 25% der Einwohner, vor allem Arbeiter und Angestellte, sind ohne gesichertes Einkommen. Auch in Frankfurt profitieren die Nationalsozialisten von der Unfähigkeit der jungen Demokratie, der Krise Herr zu werden. Viele, besonders in der Arbeiterbewegung, erkennen die Gefahr und warnen vor dem aufkommenden Faschismus.

17

17 In Frankfurt the National Socialists started their organization in the 1920s. The Stahlhelm Day of 1925 is organized by an anti-democratic union comprised of former soldiers who fought in World War I.
18 Around 1930 many inhabitants of Frankfurt suffer from poverty. A soup kitchen for the unemployed in the Friedrich Ebert quarter, 1932.
19 Anti-Nazi demonstration in Frankfurt organized by the Eiserne Front, an association of several left-wing organizations.

17 Auch in Frankfurt organisieren sich die antidemokratischen Kräfte schon in den zwanziger Jahren. Aufmarsch des 'Stahlhelms', einer Organisation ehemaliger Soldaten des Ersten Weltkrieges. 1925.
18 Um 1930 sind viele Einwohner Frankfurts sehr arm. Suppenküche für Arbeitslose in der Friedrich-Ebert-Siedlung. 1932.
19 Demonstration der 'Eisernen Front', ein Bündnis verschiedener links orientierter Organisationen, gegen den aufkommenden Nationalsozialismus. Frankfurt a.M., Opernplatz, 1932.

18

20

In 1929 the number of Jews living in Frankfurt is about 30,000, or roughly 5.5% of the population. It is the second largest Jewish community in Germany (Berlin is first) and dates back to the Middle Ages. At the beginning of the 19th century Jews are no longer required to live in the ghetto, and the law declares them equal. Their new legal status marks the beginning of a process of social and cultural assimilation. Jewish philanthropic organizations play an important role in the development of the city. Although anti-Semitism never fully disappears, Frankfurt is – for the most part – a tolerant city. Jewish citizens are able to maintain their traditional way of life or assimilate into society at large.

1929 leben in Frankfurt etwa 30.000 Juden, über 5% der Gesamtbevölkerung. Nach Berlin hat Frankfurt die größte jüdische Gemeinde in Deutschland. Ihre Tradition reicht bis ins Mittelalter zurück. Mit der Aufhebung des Gettos Anfang des 19. Jahrhunderts und der rechtlichen Gleichstellung der Juden beginnt ein Prozess der sozialen und kulturellen Assimilation. Jüdische Stiftungen für wohltätige Zwecke bestimmen die Entwicklung der Stadt. Zwar verschwindet der Antisemitismus nie völlig, aber Toleranz und Liberalität überwiegen. Jüdische Bürger dürfen ihre traditionellen Lebensweisen und Überzeugungen bewahren.

20

21

20 In 1882 a synagogue was built on Börneplatz (Börne Square) next to a huge open-air market. Photo, 1927.
21 The Judengasse (Jews Street) in Frankfurt. When the Jews lived in the ghetto the street was closed every evening and gentiles were not allowed to enter. Circa 1872.
22 The Kölnerhof Hotel near the Frankfurt Railway Station makes it clear that Jews are unwanted guests. 1905.

20 Die 1882 neu erbaute Synagoge am Börneplatz und der Wochenmarkt, 1927.
21 Die 'Judengasse' in Frankfurt kurz vor dem Abbruch der Häuser, 1872. Als die Juden noch im Getto leben mußten, wurde die Straße abends abgesperrt und war für Nichtjuden geschlossen.
22 Antisemitisches Hinweisschild im Hotel 'Kölner Hof' am Hauptbahnhof, 1905.

22

22

The 1920s and early '30s in Germany are characterized by economic crisis, inflation and hurt pride about the country's defeat in World War I and the subsequent Treaty of Versailles. Workers lose their jobs; farmers, their land; civilians, their savings.

The National Socialist German Workers Party (NSDAP), founded in 1919, recruits more and more followers. Hitler blames not only what he calls the weak government for all problems in Germany but also the Jews.

Fascist movements want absolute power, if at all possible through 'democratic' means: in other words, as many votes as possible from the followers. The Nazis shrewdly use the apparent human need for a scapegoat. Just as some political organizations today blame specific groups for all that is wrong, Hitler blames the Jews.

Die Weimarer Republik ist gekennzeichnet von Wirtschaftskrise und Inflation. Der verlorene Krieg und der 'Versailler Friedensvertrag' verletzen den Nationalstolz vieler Deutscher. Arbeiter stehen auf der Straße, Bauern verlieren ihr Land, Sparer ihr Geld. Die 1919 gegründete 'Nationalsozialistische Deutsche Arbeiterpartei' (NSDAP) gewinnt immer mehr Anhänger. Demagogisch geschickt verstehen es die Nazis, Unzufriedenheit und Verunsicherung auszunutzen. Sie geben der Demokratie und den Juden die Schuld an allen Problemen. Hitler will die absolute Macht, wenn möglich mit Hilfe der Wähler auf demokratischem Wege. Die Nazis setzen auf das Bedürfnis nach einem Sündenbock. So wie heute einige Parteien 'die Ausländer' als Ursache allen Elends bezeichnen, bietet Hitler 'die Juden' als Schuldige an.

23 Unemployed Germans. Berlin, 1932.
24 Adolf Hitler (right) as a soldier at the battle front during World War I.
25 Nazi election campaign propaganda.

24

23 *Arbeitslose in Berlin, 1932.*
24 *Hitler (rechts) als Frontsoldat während des Ersten Weltkrieges.*
25 *Wahlkampfzug der NSDAP.*

26 NSBO, the Nazi trade union, joins in the strikes to gain support.
27 The SA is an attractive alternative for many who are unemployed.
28, 29 The right-wing political parties close ranks and become known as the Harzburger Front. Bad Harzburg, October 1931.

26 Die nationalsozialistische Betriebsorganisation NSBO beteiligt sich an Streiks, um die Arbeiter für sich zu gewinnen.
27 Die SA ist eine verlockende Alternative zum monotonen Arbeitslosenalltag.
28, 29 Oktober 1931 in Bad Harzburg: Die rechte Opposition verbündet sich (Harzburger Front).

26

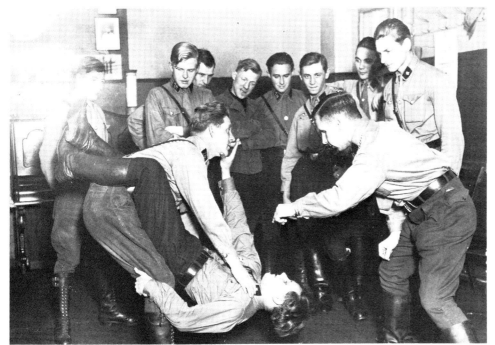

27

28

29

26

In 1932 Hitler wins the elections. He gets 37 % of the vote (13.7 million votes), and becomes the leader of a coalition government partially because the opposition is divided. On March 23, 1933, he seizes absolute power. It is essential that Hitler begins with large popular support. He is able to channel the feelings of uncertainty and discontentment into a mass political movement.
Elsewhere in Europe fascist and National Socialist movements are developing as well.

Schon 1932 stimmen 13 Mio. Menschen (37,2%) für Hitler. Die NSDAP ist damit bei weitem die stärkste Partei. Am 30.1.1933 wird Hitler zum Reichskanzler ernannt. Zwei Monate später beschließt der Reichstag das 'Ermächtigungsgesetz'. Von nun an kann Hitler ohne das Parlament regieren. Sein Erfolg läßt in ganz Europa ähnliche Bewegungen entstehen.

30

31

30,31 *Nazi posters.*
32 *The Jewish mayor of Frankfurt, Landmann, is replaced by a Nazi, Krebs.*
33 *As of January 30, 1933, Hitler is in power. The Nazis celebrate.*
34 *The swastika flag at the town hall. Frankfurt, March 1933.*

30, 31 *Plakate der NSDAP.*
32 *Der neue Frankfurter Bürgermeister, der Nationalsozialist Krebs. Der jüdische Bürgermeister Landmann ist seines Amtes enthoben worden.*
33 *Machtübernahme am 30. Januar 1933. Die Nazis feiern ihren Sieg.*
34 *Frankfurt, März 1933: Am Rathaus hängt die Hakenkreuzfahne.*

32

33

34

14, 15 DEMOCRACY ABOLISHED

14, 15 *DIE DEMOKRATIE WIRD ABGESCHAFFT*

A doctrine of National Socialism is the 'leader principle', the open rejection of parliamentary democracy. All other political parties are forbidden, and all other political opponents are eliminated. In 1933 about 150,000 political opponents are sent to concentration camps for 're-education'. In the early years of the Hitler regime elections are organized for the sake of appearance only.

Eines der wesentlichen Merkmale des Nationalsozialismus ist das Führerprinzip und die offene Ablehnung der Demokratie. Nur der Form halber werden in den ersten Jahren des Hitlerregimes noch Wahlen abgehalten.
Alle anderen politischen Parteien werden verboten, politisch Andersdenkende verfolgt. 1933 verschwinden ca. 150.000 politische Gegner in Konzentrationslagern zur sogenannten 'Umerziehung'.

35 Hitler addresses the Reichstag. October 6, 1939.
36 Even deceased democrats are enemies. The monument for Friedrich Ebert, the first president of Germany, is demolished. April, 1933.
37 Oranienburg concentration camp near Berlin. April 6, 1933.

35 Adolf Hitler während einer Rede vor dem Reichstag am 6. Oktober 1939.
36 Auch tote Demokraten sind Staatsfeinde: April 1933 wird in Frankfurt das Denkmal zu Ehren des ersten Reichspräsidenten der Weimarer Republik, Friedrich Ebert, gestürzt.
37 Konzentrationslager Oranienburg in der Nähe Berlins, 6. April 1933.

36

35

37

30

The Nazis try very quickly to dispand the labor movement. The arrest of 10,000 active members in March 1933 is a heavy blow to the trade unions. In spite of terror and repression, anti-Nazi trade union groups get 80% of the vote during company elections that same month.

On May 1, 1933, Hitler announces the celebration of the 'Day of National Labor'. The largest trade union ADGB, calls on its members to participate. It turns into a mass Nazi manifestation, however. On May 2nd the Nazis occupy the trade union buildings and seize property. Trade union leaders are replaced by Nazis. The DAF (German Workers Front) is the only union allowed to operate as of May 10, 1933. All workers are forced to become members. There is no place for an independent labor movement that protects the interests of its members. Workers and employers must cooperate. Strikes are forbidden.

Die Arbeiterbewegung ist eines der ersten Angriffsziele der Nazis. Im März 1933 werden 10.000 aktive Mitglieder verhaftet. Doch trotz des NS-Terrors erringen die freien Gewerkschaften bei den Betriebsratswahlen 80% der Stimmen. Obwohl Hitler den 1. Mai zum 'Tag der nationalen Arbeit' ausruft, fordert der 'Allgemeine Deutsche Gewerkschaftsbund', ADGB, zur Teilnahme auf. Er hofft, daß der Feiertag der Arbeiterbewegung zu einer Antinazidemonstration wird. Doch Regie führen die Nazis. Der Tag wird zu einer gigantischen NS-Veranstaltung. Am folgenden Tag besetzen die Nationalsozialisten die Gewerkschaftsgebäude und beschlagnahmen das Eigentum der freien Gewerkschaften. Am 10. Mai wird die 'Deutsche Arbeitsfront' als Pflichtverband für alle Arbeiter gegründet. Das ist das Ende der freien Gewerkschaftsbewegung.

39

40

38 *Communists and Social Democrats are arrested by the SA. Spring 1933.*
39 *Throughout Germany millions of people celebrate the Day of National Labor on May 1, 1933. Munich.*
40 *On May 2, 1933, the SA seizes trade union buildings throughout the country. Berlin.*

38 *Frühjahr 1933: Viele Kommunisten und Sozialdemokraten werden verhaftet. Die SA tritt als Hilfspolizei auf.*
39 *München, 1. Mai 1933: Zum 'Tag der Arbeit' inszenieren die Nazis in ganz Deutschland riesige Massenveranstaltungen.*
40 *2. Mai 1933: Wie hier in Berlin besetzt die SA im ganzen Land die Gewerkschaftshäuser.*

32

To fight the vast unemployment, the Nazis initiate employment projects: construction of freeways (Autobahnen) and fortification of the arms industry. The country's economy changes to a war economy. To that end everyone must contribute. Teen-agers and young adults are forced to work an allotted period of time for a nominal fee. Simultaneously, they are indoctrinated in Nazi ideology. From 1938 on, workers in certain professions are forced to work in the war industry.

Gegen die große Arbeitslosigkeit setzen die Nazis Arbeitsbeschaffungsprogramme: z.B. den Autobahnbau oder Kriegsgüterproduktion. Im Januar 1933 wird der Arbeitsdienst für alle Jugendlichen zur gesetzlichen Pflicht. Gegen minimales Entgelt wird schwere Arbeit verlangt und im nationalsozialistischen Sinne erzogen. Ab 1938 werden Facharbeiter der verschiedensten Berufe verpflichtet, in der Rüstungsindustrie zu arbeiten.

41 On behalf of 40,000 male and 2,000 female labor serviceworkers, their leader pledges allegiance to Hitler. September 1938.
42 Workers marching to work.
43 Handing out shovels to build the freeways. Near Frankfurt. September 1933.

41 September 1938. Im Namen von 40.000 Arbeitern und 2.000 Arbeiterinnen schwört Reichsarbeitsleiter Hierl Hitler die Treue.
42 Kolonnenweise marschieren die Arbeiter zu einer Autobahnbaustelle in der Nähe Frankfurts.
43 Schaufeln für den Autobahnbau werden verteilt. Frankfurt, 23. September 1933.

42

43

18, 19 THE ANTI-JEWISH BOYCOTT AND POPULAR ANTI-SEMITISM

18, 19 DER ANTIJÜDISCHE BOYKOTT UND SPONTANER ANTISEMITISMUS

On April 1, 1933, Joseph Goebbels declares the official boycott of Jewish shopkeepers, doctors and lawyers.

On April 11, 1933, all public servants with at least one Jewish grandparent are fired. These and scores of other measures are designed to remove Jews from their jobs and businesses. According to the Nazi philosophy, there is only room for pure white Germans ('Aryans') in the nation. Only Aryans can be 'compatriots' (Volksgenossen). Jewish companies are 'Aryanized': the Nazis force Jewish business owners to sell their property, and the Nazis themselves fire the Jewish personnel.

Propagandaminister Joseph Goebbels verkündet für den 1. April 1933 den Boykott jüdischer Geschäfte, Ärzte und Rechtsanwälte. Doch das ist nur der Anfang der anti-jüdischen Maßnahmen. Am 11. April werden alle Beamten, die mindestens ein jüdisches Großelternteil haben, aus dem Staatsdienst entlassen. Immer mehr Berufe werden für Juden verboten. Nur sogenannte 'Arier' gelten als 'Volksgenossen'.

Die nationalsozialistische Rassenlehre bestimmt, wer Deutscher sein darf und wer nicht. Jüdische Betriebe und Unternehmen werden 'arisiert', die Besitzer enteignet, das jüdische Personal entlassen.

46

45

47

48

44, 46, 47 Appeals to boycott
Jewish-owned shops.
45 'Jew'. Berlin, 1933.
48 A Jewish shopkeeper wearing his
military decorations in front of his
store in Cologne.

44, 46, 47 Boykottpropaganda gegen
jüdische Geschäfte.
45 Berlin, 1933.
48 Ein jüdischer Kaufmann mit
seinen Orden aus dem Ersten Weltkrieg vor seinem Kölner Geschäft.

49, 50 *Carnival in Cologne, 1934. Men dress up as Jews. 'The last Jews disappear. We're only on a short trip to Lichtenstein or Jaffa'. 1934.*
51 *Carnival wagon with men in concentration camp uniforms: 'Away to Dachau'. Nuremberg, 1936.*
52 *At the Nuremberg carnival in 1938. 'National enemies'. A puppet at the gallows wearing a Star of David.*

49

50

51

49, 50 *Karneval in Köln, 1934.*
51 *Karnevalszug in Nürnberg, 1936.*
52 *Karneval in Nürnberg 1938:
Wagen mit dem Motto 'Volksschäd-
linge'.*

52

20 THE NATIONAL SOCIALIST 'WELFARE STATE'

20 DER VÖLKISCHE 'VERSORGUNGSSTAAT'

The Nazi state gives the impression it is taking care of everything: vacations, recreation, art and culture, health care for mother and child, etc. This, however, applies only to those who are 'Volksgenossen': racially 'pure' and mentally and physically healthy.

Der NS-Staat vereinnahmt alle gesellschaftlichen Bereiche. Er kümmert sich um Freizeit und Ferien, Kunst und Kultur, Gesundheit für Mutter und Kind, verspricht jeder deutschen Familie ein Auto. In den Genuß dieser Vergünstigungen sollen allerdings nur 'reinrassige', körperlich und geistig gesunde Volksgenossen kommen.

54

55

56

53, 54, 55, 56 *The 'Kraft Durch Freude' (Strength Through Joy) organization promises vacations and entertainment for every German: a trip to Madeira or Libya, to the mountains to ski or the beach to swim. Even the famous Fratellini clowns perform for Kraft Durch Freude in the Horst Wessel Hospital. Kraft Durch Freude organizes vacations for one million Germans.*

53, 54, 55, 56 *'Des Führers Werk hat es ermöglicht.' Die Freizeitorganisation der Deutschen Arbeitsfront 'Kraft durch Freude' verspricht allen Deutschen Urlaub und Entspannung: eine Reise nach Madeira oder in die lybische Wüste. Geboten werden Wintersport wie Strandferien. Selbst die weltberühmten Clowns 'Die Fratelinis' treten für 'Kraft durch Freude' im Berliner Horst-Wessel-Krankenhaus auf. Eine Million Deutsche machen auf diese Weise erstmals Urlaub.*

40

The Nazis believe that a healthy nation should not spend money on the mentally handicapped. Consequently, thousands of mentally handicapped are quietly killed beginning in 1939. In contrast to their silence about the Jews, the churches voice indignation and protest over the killing of the mentally handicapped. The so-called Euthanasia Project is stopped in 1941. A total of 72,000 physically and mentally handicapped men, women and children and alcoholics are killed by injection or gas.

In the last years of the Hitler regime another 130,000 patients die of starvation or cold.because of deliberate neglect.

Für die Nazis sind Behinderte 'lebensunwertes Leben'. Ab 1939 werden heimlich tausende Behinderte ermordet. Im Gegensatz zur Judenverfolgung ruft dies Empörung und Protest, vor allem bei den Kirchen, hervor. 1941 wird das sogenannte 'Euthanasie-programm' größtenteils eingestellt. Bis zu diesem Zeitpunkt sind bereits ca. 72.000 geistig und körperlich Behinderte sowie Alkoholiker durch Injektionen und Vergasung umgebracht worden. In den letzten Kriegsjahren sterben weitere 130.000 Patienten an Hunger und Kälte.

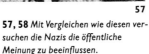

57

58

57, 58 *With comparisons like these, the Nazis try to influence public opinion: 'A genetically healthy family is forced to live in an old railroad car.' 'Hereditarily mentally handicapped people in an institution.' From 'Little Handbook for Heredity and Race Sciences.' 1934.*

57, 58 *Mit Vergleichen wie diesen ver-suchen die Nazis die öffentliche Meinung zu beeinflussen.*

59

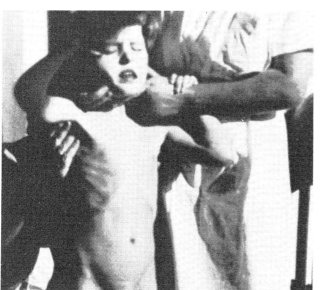

60

59 The mental institution in Hadamar. The corpses of more than 10,000 victims are burned in the crematorium.
60 This mentally handicapped girl is being photographed before she is killed.

59 Die psychiatrische Klinik in Hadamar. Die sterblichen Überreste von mehr als 10.000 Opfern werden im Krematorium verbrannt.
60 Dieses geistig behinderte Mädchen wird noch fotographiert, bevor es umgebracht wird.

42

The Nazis encourage large families. More children mean more future soldiers. But these children must be racially 'pure' and healthy. On June 14, 1933, a law is introduced 'to prevent genetically unfit offspring.' The result: forced sterilization for individuals who are mentally handicapped, epileptic, deaf or blind.
1935: the Nuremberg laws 'protect German blood and German honor' by forbidding marriage between Jews and Aryans and by punishing Jews and Aryans who engage in sexual intercourse.
1937: the Gestapo (Nazi police) brings 385 black German children to university hospitals to be sterilized.

Die Nazis fördern kinderreiche Familien: je mehr Kinder, desto mehr Soldaten. Aber die Kinder müssen hundertprozentig gesund sowie 'rassenrein' sein. Um dies sicherzustellen, wird am 14. Juli 1933 das 'Gesetz zur Verhütung erbkranken Nachwuchses' in Kraft gesetzt. Zur Pflicht werden u.a. die Sterilisation bei erblicher Geisteskrankheit, Epilepsie, Taub- und Blindheit. 1935 folgen die Nürnberger Gesetze 'Zum Schutze des deutschen Blutes und der deutschen Ehre'. Sie verbieten Ehen zwischen 'Ariern' und Juden und stellen Geschlechtsverkehr zwischen ihnen unter Strafe. 1937 bringt die Gestapo 385 farbige deutsche Kinder zur Sterilisation in Universitätskliniken.

61

62

63

64

61, 62, 63, 64 'This is how a German mother looks, and this is a non-German alien mother.' (. . .) 'These are children of your own blood, and these belong to an alien race'. From the SS booklet 'Victory of Arms, Victory of Children'.
65 'Day of Large Families'. Frankfurt, 1937.

61, 62, 63, 64 '. . . läßt uns die tiefste Bestimmung der deutschen Frau ahnen, nämlich die, Mutter vieler gesunder Kinder zu sein.' – National-sozialistische Frauenpolitik.
65 Frankfurt 1937: 'Reichstag der Kinderreichen'.

65

44

Although the Nazi ideology is basically anti-Christian, from 1933 on the Nazis can count on ample support from the German churches. With few exceptions both the Protestant and Catholic churches endorse the racial and political priciples of the Nazis.

On March 28, 1933, the Catholic bishops declare their loyalty to Hitler. The next month the Protestant Altpreussische Union also endorses Hitler.

During elections in the Evangical Church on July 25, 1933, the anti-Semitic 'German Christians' capture a large majority. The official churches fail to protest against the persecution of the Jews, even Jews who had converted to Christianity.

Obwohl die Nazi-Ideologie in ihrem Wesen antichristlich ist, erfreuen sich die Nazis dennoch breiter Unterstützung der deutschen Kirchen. Bis auf wenige Ausnahmen stellen sich sowohl die katholische als auch die protestantische Kirche hinter die Staats- und Rassenlehren. Schon am 28. März erklären die katholischen Bischöfe Hitler gegenüber ihre Treue. Bei den Wahlen innerhalb der evangelischen Kirche am 25. Juli 1933 erreichen die antisemitischen 'Deutschen Christen' eine große Mehrheit. Von offiziellen Kirchenstellen beider Glaubensgemeinschaften hört man kein Wort des Protestes gegen die Judenverfolgung. Selbst getaufte Juden werden im Stich gelassen.

66 Bishop Müller, speaking in Berlin, September 25, 1934.
67 Festival for the Catholic youth in Berlin, August 20, 1933: 'Long live the Führer!'
68 Hildegard Schaeder is a member of the 'Bekennende Kirche' to which Dietrich Bonhoeffer and Martin Niemöller also belong. Unlike the official churches, this group protests from the very beginning against the persecution of the Jews. Mrs. Schaeder helps Jews leave Germany. Between 1943 and 1945 she is detained in Ravensbrück concentration camp.

67

66 Reichsbischof Müller spricht im Berliner Lustgarten, 25. September 1934.
67 Treffen der katholischen Jugend in Berlin, 20. August 1933: 'Lang lebe der Führer.'
68 Trotz der Zusammenarbeit zwischen Nazis und Kirchenführung gibt es auch in den Kirchen Widerstand gegen das NS-Regime. Er manifestiert sich u.a. in der 'Bekennenden Kirche', die gegen die Judenverfolgung protestiert. Zu ihren bekanntesten Mitgliedern gehören Martin Niemöller und Dietrich Bonhoeffer. Hildegard Schaeder versorgt Juden und hilft ihnen bei der Flucht. Dafür stecken sie die Nazis von 1943 bis 1945 in das KZ Ravensbrück.

68

66

Beginning in 1933 only one youth movement is allowed: the Hitler Youth (Hitler Jugend). All other organizations are either incorporated or forbidden. The aim is to convert youth into National Socialists. For boys the emphasis is on military training; for girls, motherhood.
The youth movement focuses on sports and physical activities. Reading and learning are of secondary importance.

Ab 1933 gibt es in Deutschland nur noch eine einzige offizielle Jugendorganisation: die 'Hitlerjugend'. Alle anderen sind in ihr aufgegangen oder verboten.
Ziel ist, die Jugendlichen zu überzeugten Nationalsozialisten zu formen. Bei den Jungen überwiegt das militärische Training. Mädchen werden auf die Mutterschaft vorbereitet. Schwerpunkte der 'Hitlerjugend' sind Sport und körperliche Bewegung. Auf Lesen und Lernen wird wenig Wert gelegt.

70

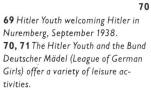

69 *Hitler Youth welcoming Hitler in Nuremberg, September 1938.*
70, 71 *The Hitler Youth and the Bund Deutscher Mädel (League of German Girls) offer a variety of leisure activities.*
72 *League of German Girls sports festival in Frankfurt, 1938.*

69 *Nürnberg, September 1938.*
Die 'HJ' grüßt Hitler.
70, 71 *Die 'Hitlerjugend' (HJ) und der 'Bund Deutscher Mädel' (BDM), organisieren attraktive Freizeitgestaltung.*
72 *Sportfest des 'BDM' in Frankfurt, 1938.*

69

72

48

Education becomes National Socialist-oriented.
In April 1933 a law is passed to fire all teachers who are Jews or political opponents. Hundreds of textbooks are replaced by Nazi-written material. New subjects, such as genetics and the study of race and nation, are introduced.
The universities replace professors. Political opponents and Jews are stripped of their academic titles. The number of Jewish and female students is limited.
In 1938 Jews are barred from schools and universities altogether.

Im NS-Staat wird das gesamte Bildungssystem an der Nazi-Ideologie ausgerichtet. Im April 1933 wird ein Gesetz erlassen, um alle politischen Gegner und Juden aus dem Schuldienst und von den Hochschulen zu entlassen. Schulbücher werden durch nationalsozialistisches Lehrmaterial ersetzt, neue Pflichtfächer wie Erblichkeitslehre, Rassen- und Völkerkunde eingeführt. Die Zahl der jüdischen und weiblichen Studenten an den Universitäten wird begrenzt. 1938 wird Juden der Besuch von Hochschulen gänzlich verboten.

74

75

73 Schoolchildren learn the Hitler salute.
74 Eugen Fischer, Chancellor of the University of Berlin, is replaced by Wilhelm Krüger, who wears the traditional robe over his Nazi uniform. 1935.
75 Die 'Weisse Rose' (The White Rose) is a resistance organization in Munich, 1942. Hans and Sophie Scholl, brother and sister, are active members. They are caught by the Gestapo and executed after a quick trial. Anti-Nazi student groups such as these spring up in various German university towns.

73 Schulkinder grüßen ihre Lehrerin mit dem Hitlergruß.
74 Rektorenwechsel an der Friedrich-Wilhelm-Universität Berlin, April 1935. Nachfolger von Eugen Fischer wird Wilhelm Krüger. Er stellt ganz offen seine politische Gesinnung zur Schau.
75 München 1942. Die studentische Widerstandsgruppe 'Weiße Rose', um Hans und Sophie Scholl, verteilt Flugblätter gegen das NS-Regime. Die Gestapo spürt sie auf, verhaftet ihre Mitglieder. Im Schnellverfahren werden die Geschwister Scholl und ihre Mitkämpfer zum Tode verurteilt und hingerichtet. In anderen Universitätsstädten bilden sich ähnliche Widerstandsgruppen.

50

Nazism is dependent upon propaganda. Mass meetings, photos, posters, stamps – they all are used to propagate the Nazi ideology. Nazis consider propaganda so important they even create a special Ministry of Propaganda under the leadership of Goebbels.

Der Nationalsozialismus lebt von der Propaganda. Massenversammlungen, Fotos, Plakate: alles dient ein und demselben Ziel: der Verbreitung nationalsozialistischen Gedankengutes. Das Reichspropagandaministerium unter Joseph Goebbels übernimmt Leitung, Lenkung und Koordination.

76 A swastika flag for every household.
77 The annual 'Day of the Party', a gigantic propaganda meeting. 1937.
78 Propaganda from the magazine Stürmer: 'The Jews Are Our Misfortune'.

76 Für jede deutsche Familie eine Hakenkreuzfahne.
77 Die jährlichen 'Reichsparteitage' in Nürnberg sind gigantische Propagandakundgebungen. 1937.
78 'Stürmer'-Werbekasten, Gaubereich Worms.

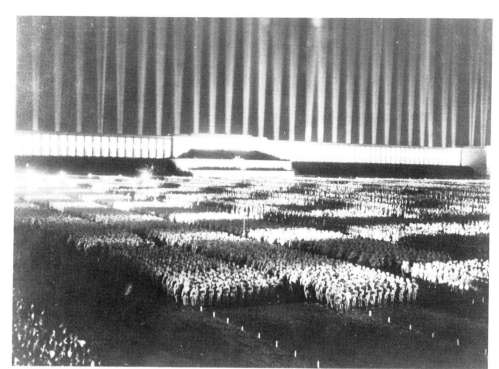

77

76

78

In Hitler's Germany art and culture are made totally subordinate to the Nazi ideology. All works of art by Jews and political opponents are destroyed or confiscated and henceforth forbidden.
The independent artist can no longer work. Painters, musicians and authors are forced to join Goebbels' 'chamber of culture' in order to continue working.

Das gesamte Kulturleben wird der Nazi-Ideologie unterworfen. Werke jüdischer und politisch unliebsamer Künstler werden verboten, vernichtet oder beschlagnahmt. Freischaffenden Künstlern wird die Arbeit unmöglich gemacht.
Jeder Künstler muß der neu gegründeten 'Reichskulturkammer' beitreten. Nichtmitgliedern wird jegliche künstlerische Betätigung verboten.

79

79 *Artists are forced to choose between leaving the country or adapting to the new situation. Film director Leni Riefenstahl (center) puts her skills to use for the Nazis. Her famous propaganda movie is 'Triumph des Willens' (Victory of the Will), a documentary of the Nazi Party Day in Nuremberg, 1935.*
80, 81, 82 *The burning of banned books in Berlin. May 1933.*

79 *Künstlern bleibt nur die Wahl zwischen Auswanderung, Anpassung oder Berufsaufgabe. Die Filmregisseurin Leni Riefenstahl stellt sich völlig in den Dienst des NS-Regimes. Ihre bekannteste Arbeit: der Propagandafilm 'Triumph des Willens', gedreht auf dem NSDAP-Parteitag 1935.*
80, 81, 82 *Bücherverbrennung, Mai 1933.*

80

81

82

54

Shortly after coming to power, Hitler meets with the top echelon of the German Army to propose his plans. The 'Shame of Versailles' must be erased. Rearmament, return of the lost territories and new 'space to live' (Lebensraum) in the east are his goals. The army is willing on one condition: that the power of the SA, Hitler's paramilitary organization consisting of 2.5 million men, is limited. On Hitler's orders, the top leaders of the SA are murdered on June 30, 1934.

At the end of 1934 the army swears its oath of loyalty to Hitler personally. In 1935 the draft is introduced.

Wenige Tage nach der Machtübernahme trifft Hitler mit der Heeresleitung zusammen, um seine militärischen Pläne bekanntzugeben. An erster Stelle steht dabei die Wiederaufrüstung Deutschlands und die Zurückeroberung der im 1. Weltkrieg verlorenen Gebiete. Zusätzlich soll 'Lebensraum' im Osten gewonnen werden. Die Heeresleitung stimmt zu unter der Voraussetzung, daß Hitler die Macht der paramilitärischen SA, eines lästigen Konkurrenten, beschneidet. Am 30. Juni 1934 wird auf Befehl Hitlers die gesamte SA-Leitung von der SS liquidiert. 1935 wird die allgemeine Wehrpflicht wiedereingeführt.

83 General Ludwig Beck resigns in 1938 after learning of Hitler's plan to attack Czechoslovakia. Later, Beck is involved in the attempted murder of Hitler on July 20, 1944. When the attack fails, he commits suicide.
84 The first group of new recruits. June 1935.
85 The arms industry in full action. Between 1934 and 1939 more than 60 billion German Marks are spent on armaments. For social services only 4 billlion Marks are available.

83 Generaloberst Ludwig Beck tritt 1938 aus Protest gegen Angriffspläne gegen die Tschechoslowakei zurück. Später beteiligt er sich am mißglückten Attentat auf Hitler am 20. Juli 1944, wird verhaftet und zum Selbstmord getrieben.
84 Der erste Jahrgang neuer Rekruten, Juni 1935.
85 Die Rüstungsindustrie arbeitet auf Hochtouren. Zwischen 1934 und 1939 werden rund 60 Milliarden Reichsmark in die Rüstung gesteckt. Gleichzeitig sinken die Sozialausgaben. Im gleichen Zeitraum werden für Sozialausgaben nur 4 Mrd. RM aufgewendet.

83

84

85

56

In April 1933 Adolf Hitler receives a delegation of German judges. Although the judges dedicate themselves to the new order, they ask that in return for their loyalty, Hitler agree to guarantee their independence. Hitler does agree, provided certain 'necessary measures' are taken. The delegation approves his measures, and as a result, Jews and political opponents are fired.

A few judges realize the ramifications and retire. Other judges believe that by staying on, worse situations can be prevented. Soon, however, the judicial system becomes part of the terror machinery. To begin with, the judges accept the race laws and evidence obtained by torture. Then they accept the unrestricted actions of the SA, SS and Gestapo against so-called traitors. And finally, they even accept that Jews, homosexuals and gypsies are being stripped of any rights.

Am 7. April 1933 empfängt Hitler eine Delegation der deutschen Richterschaft. Sie bieten ihm ihre Unterstützung an, bitten jedoch um Bestätigung der richterlichen Unabhängigkeit. Hitler gewährt diese unter bestimmten Voraussetzungen: Entfernung der Juden sowie aller politischen Gegner aus dem Justizapparat. Die Säuberung der Justiz stößt kaum auf Widerstand. Nur wenige Richter legen ihr Amt aus Protest nieder. Viele bleiben in der Überzeugung, so Schlimmeres verhüten zu können. Der Rest sind überzeugte Nazis.

Binnen kurzer Zeit steht der gesamte Rechtsapparat im Dienst des Nationalsozialismus. Die Justiz akzeptiert die Rassengesetze. Durch Folter erzwungene Geständnisse gelten als Beweismittel. Selbstjustiz durch SA, SS und Gestapo werden stillschweigend toleriert. Widerstandslos wird hingenommen, daß bestimmte Bevölkerungsgruppen wie Juden, Roma und Sinti oder Homosexuelle völlig entrechtet werden.

86 Street control in Berlin, 1933.
87 A member of the SA (right) serves as a police officer. The original caption of this photo reads: 'Law and order restored in the streets of Berlin.'
88 The SA in action. Their victims have no rights.
89 The 'Volksgerichtshof' (People's Court of Justice) with President Roland Freisler condemned hundreds of people to capital punishment, sometimes for very minor offences.

86 Straßenkontrolle in Berlin, 1933.
87 Ein SA-Mann als Polizist. Der Originaltext zu diesem Foto lautet: 'Ruhe und Ordnung sind wiederhergestellt in den Straßen Berlins.'
88 Die SA in Aktion. Ihre Opfer sind machtlos.
89 Der 'Volksgerichtshof' unter Vorsitz von Roland Freisler verurteilt hunderte zum Tode, häufig für die kleinsten Vergehen.

87

88

89

58

In 1933 about half a million Jews (or 0.77% of the population) live in Germany, in the cities and throughout the countryside. As soon as the Nazis come to power the Jews are systematically isolated. By April 1933 Jewish civil servants are already being dismissed. In all aspects of life – work, education, leisure time, culture – the Jews are separated from the non-Jews via a seemingly endless list of decrees. The ever shrinking Jewish community tries to continue normal life as much as possible against all odds.

1933 wohnen in Deutschland ca. 500.000 Juden (0,77% der Gesamtbevölkerung). Nachdem die Nazis an die Macht gekommen sind, werden die Juden Schritt für Schritt entrechtet und isoliert. Schon im April 1933 werden jüdische Beamte entlassen. Mittels einer schier endlosen Reihe von Verordnungen werden Juden und Nichtjuden in immer mehr Lebensbereichen voneinander getrennt: bei Arbeit, Ausbildung, Freizeit, Familie usw. Die kleiner werdende jüdische Gemeinschaft versucht dem zu begegnen, indem sie sich bemüht, so normal wie möglich weiterzuleben.

90 *A farewell. Teacher Ruth Ehrmann saying goodbye to a pupil who is going to emigrate.*

90 *Abschied: Lehrerin Ruth Ehrmann verabschiedet einen Schüler, bevor er das Land verläßt.*

90

91

92

91 The Jewish Cultural Union offers the opportunity for performers and musicians who have been dismissed to continue to practice their profession – but only for Jewish audiences. Grünewald, 1935.
92 Letters from family members and friends provide the only contact with those who have left the country. 1938.
93 The youth section of the Jewish sports club Maccabee.

91 Der 'Jüdische Kulturbund' bietet jüdischen Künstlern die Möglichkeit, ihrem Beruf auch weiterhin nachzugehen – jedoch nur für jüdisches Publikum.
92 Briefe von Familienmitgliedern und Freunden sind der einzige Kontakt mit denen, die Deutschland verlassen haben. 1938.
93 Die Jugendabteilung des jüdischen Sportvereins 'Makkabi'. Berlin, 1936.

93

60

On November 9-11, 1938, scores of synagogues and thousands of Jewish-owned shops all over Germany and Austria are ransacked and burned. This is known as 'Crystal Night', named after the shattered glass windows which were a result of the rampage. Starting November 12 the first mass arrests of Jews take place. About 30,000 Jewish men and boys are taken and deported to the Buchenwald, Dachau and Sachsenhausen concentration camps. The *'Kristallnacht'* signifies an important, stepped-up persecution of the Jews.

Zwischen dem 9. und 11. November 1938 werden in ganz Deutschland und Österreich dutzende Synagogen in Brand gesteckt und tausende jüdischer Läden verwüstet. Rund 30.000 Jungen und Männer werden in die Konzentrationslager Buchenwald, Dachau und Sachsenhausen verschleppt. Von nun an wird die Verfolgung der Juden schnell vorangetrieben.

94 *Jewish shops with shattered windows.*
95 *Frankfurt's synagogue afire, Börneplatz (Börne Square). November 9, 1938.*
96 *Burning the synagogue's furniture in Tiengen. November 10, 1938.*

94 *Jüdische Läden nach der 'Kristallnacht'.*
95 *Börneplatz, 9. November 1938. Die Frankfurter Synagoge geht in Flammen auf.*
96 *Verbrennen des Synagogeninventars in Tiengen, 10. November 1938.*

95

96

From 1933 on more and more Jews leave Germany, but Kristallnacht in 1938 triggers a mass exodus. By the spring of 1939 about half of Germany's 500,000 Jews have left. The problem for Jews is where to go.

Jewish refugees are not welcome everywhere. Many countries quickly place a quota on the number of Jews they allow to enter. In some cases, countries even close their borders to Jews.

As a result, German-Jewish refugees are scattered throughout the world, sometimes through bizarre and roundabout ways.

Ab 1933 entschließen sich immer mehr Juden dazu, Deutschland zu verlassen. 1938, insbesondere nach der 'Reichskristallnacht', steigt der Strom jüdischer Flüchtlinge stark an. Im Frühjahr 1939 hat rund die Hälfte der etwa 500.000 deutschen Juden das Reich verlassen. Sie sind keineswegs überall willkommen. Viele Länder beschränken den Zuzug jüdischer Emigranten. Häufig werden die Grenzen sogar ganz geschlossen. So kommt es, daß die deutschen Juden über die ganze Welt verstreut werden.

97

97

97 *A travel agency on Meineke Street. Berlin, 1939.*
98, 99 *From 1938 onward, many Jewish parents in Germany and Austria send their children to other countries that might be safer.*
100 *Arrival of Jewish refugees in Shanghai. By 1940 about 20,000 are allowed to settle there.*

97 *Auswanderungswillige vor einem Reisebüro in der Meinekestraße, Berlin 1939.*
98, 99 *Wegen der zunehmenden Verfolgung versuchen immer mehr jüdische Bürger in Deutschland und Österreich, ihre Kinder im Ausland in Sicherheit zu bringen.*
100 *Ankunft jüdischer Flüchtlinge in Shanghai. 1940 dürfen etwa 20.000 Juden einreisen.*

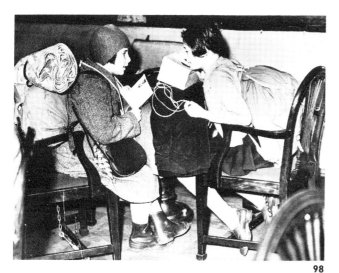

98

99

100

64

The reactions from other countries to the Nazi regime differ markedly. Many do not believe Hitler will stay in power for a long time and do not want to get involved. Others strongly oppose the developments in Germany. Still others are so enthusiastic about Hitler they organize National Socialist movements in their own country. In general, the danger of National Socialism and the persecution of the Jews is underestimated.

Hitlers Regierung löst im Ausland unterschiedliche Reaktionen aus. Viele können sich überhaupt nicht vorstellen, daß die Nazis länger an der Macht bleiben. Andere protestieren gegen das NS-Regime. Einige bejubeln den Sieg des Nationalsozialismus und gründen im eigenen Land NS-Verbände. Im allgemeinen jedoch werden der Nationalsozialismus und das Ausmaß der Judenverfolgung stark unterschätzt.

102

103

101 As a protest against the mass arrests of socialists and communists in Germany, 18-year-old Sara Roth chains herself to a street lamp. Washington, D.C., 1933.
102 A plea to open Palestine to Jewish refugees. London, November 1938.
103 In many countries organizations sympathetic to the Nazi's are founded. A branch of the SA is formed in California.

101 Washington, 1933: Sarah Roth (18 Jahre) kettet sich an eine Laterne, um gegen die massenhaften Verhaftungen deutscher Kommunisten und Sozialisten zu protestieren.
102 London, November 1938. Schaukästen mit Protestaufrufen gegen die Judenverfolgung, sowie der Forderung nach einer Öffnung Palästinas für jüdische Flüchtlinge.
103 In vielen Ländern bilden sich NS-Sympathisantengruppen, die die NS-Ideologie übernehmen. Hier in Kalifornien, USA.

The Jewish population in Holland in 1940 is about 140,000, 24,000 of whom are refugees. The Dutch government, which is not convinced of the Jews' need to flee from Germany, restricts the number of immigrants allowed into Holland.
The only assistance available to refugees is in camps like Westerbork, for which the Dutch Jewish community is required to pay all costs.
Amsterdam has the largest Jewish community: 90,000. Most are poor. They work in the trade, garment and diamond industries. Although there are expressions of anti-Semitism, most Jews feel they have assimilated into the Dutch community.

1940 zählen die Niederlande 140.000 jüdische Einwohner, darunter 24.000 Flüchtlinge aus Deutschland. Die Regierung verfolgt eine sehr strikte Flüchtlingspolitik, da sie von der Notwendigkeit zur Flucht aus dem Deutschen Reich nicht überzeugt ist. Hilfeleistungen beschränken sich auf Auffanglager wie das Barackenlager Westerbork. Die Kosten hat die jüdische Gemeinde zu tragen.
Amsterdam hat bei weitem die größte jüdische Gemeinde: rund 90.000 Menschen. Die meisten sind arm. Viele arbeiten im Handel oder in der Diamanten- und Bekleidungsindustrie. Obwohl es antisemitische Äußerungen gibt, fühlen sich die meisten Juden in die niederländischen Gesellschaft integriert.

104

104 Uilenburg, a street in the Jewish quarter in Amsterdam.
105 Matzo bakery in the Jewish quarter in Amsterdam.
106 The Waterloo Square market located in the center of the Jewish quarter, Amsterdam.
107 Jews at work in the diamond industry.

104 Uilenburg, eine Straße im Amsterdamer Judenviertel.
105 Matze-Bäcker im Amsterdamer Judenviertel.
106 In den Diamantenschleifereien arbeiten viele Juden.
107 Der Waterlooplatzmarkt in Amsterdam mitten im jüdischen Viertel.

105

106

107

36-43 THE FRANK FAMILY – HOLLAND, 1933-1940

36-43 DIE FAMILIE FRANK – DIE NIEDERLANDE 1933-1940

In 1933, after Hitler comes to power and after the anti-Jewish boycott, Otto Frank leaves Frankfurt for Amsterdam. He starts a branch of the German Opekta Co. there, and soon Edith, Margot and Anne join him.

The Frank family moves into a house on Merwedeplein in the southern part of the city. Anne and Margot attend the Montessori School nearby. They have lots of friends, and photographs are proof of the many excursions they took. The Franks become good friends with some other Jewish emigrants who settle in the same neighborhood. The Opekta Co. is doing rather well.

However, this relatively carefree life is suddenly interrupted by the German invasion in May 1940.

Als Hitler 1933 an die Macht kommt, verläßt Otto Frank Deutschland und geht nach Amsterdam. Hier eröffnet er eine Filiale der deutschen Firma Opekta. Schon bald folgen ihm Edith, Margot und Anne in die Niederlande.

Die Familie findet in Amsterdam-Süd, am Merwedeplein, eine Wohnung. Hier wachsen Anne und Margot auf.

Sie gehen beide auf die in der Nähe gelegene Montessori-Schule, haben viele Freundinnen und machen oft Ausflüge.

In diesem Viertel wohnen viele jüdische Emigranten. Mit einigen freundet sich die Familie Frank gut an. Die Geschäfte der Firma Opekta laufen verhältnismäßig gut. Doch der deutsche Einmarsch im Mai 1940 macht dem ungestörten Leben ein Ende.

108

109

108, 109 *Anne with her friend Sanne Ledermann, 1935, on Merwedeplein, Amsterdam.*
110, 111 *Summer 1934.*
112 *Anne with a girl friend, 1934.*

108, 109 *Anne mit ihrer Freundin Sanne auf dem Merwedeplein in Amsterdam.*
110, 111 *Sommer 1934.*
112 *Anne mit einer Freundin, Juli 1934.*

110

111

112

113

113 *Anne attends a Montessori school, 1935.*
114 *In Amstelrust Park with a rabbit, 1938.*

113 *Anne auf der Montessori-Schule, 1935.*
114 *Im Amstelrustpark, mit einem Kaninchen, 1938.*

114

115

115 *Anne's 10th birthday. June 12, 1939 (Anne, second from left).*
116 *Anne.*
117 *Margot, a girl friend and Anne on the beach at Middelkerke, Belgium. July 1937.*

115 *Anne 10. Geburtstag. 12. Juni 1939 (Anne, als Zweite von links).*
116 *Anne.*
117 *Margot, mit einer Freundin, und Anne am Strand in Middelkerke, Belgien. Juli 1939.*

116

117

118

119

118 Anne on the roof of the house on
Merwedeplein, 1940.
119 The Frank family on
Merwedeplein, May 1940.
120 Anne with Hermann and Herbert
Wilp.

118 Anne auf dem Dach des Hauses
am Merwedeplatz.
119 Die Familie Frank auf dem Merwedeplein, Mai 1940.
120 Anne mit Hermann und Herbert
Wilp.

120

122

123

121 Margot and Anne, 1940.
122 On the beach in Zandvoort,
August 1940.
123 Anne. 1940.

121 Margot und Anne, 1940.
122 In Zandvoort am Strand,
August 1940.
123 Anne, 1940.

121

1935

1935

1936

1937

1938

1939

1940

1941

1942

125 *Anne.*

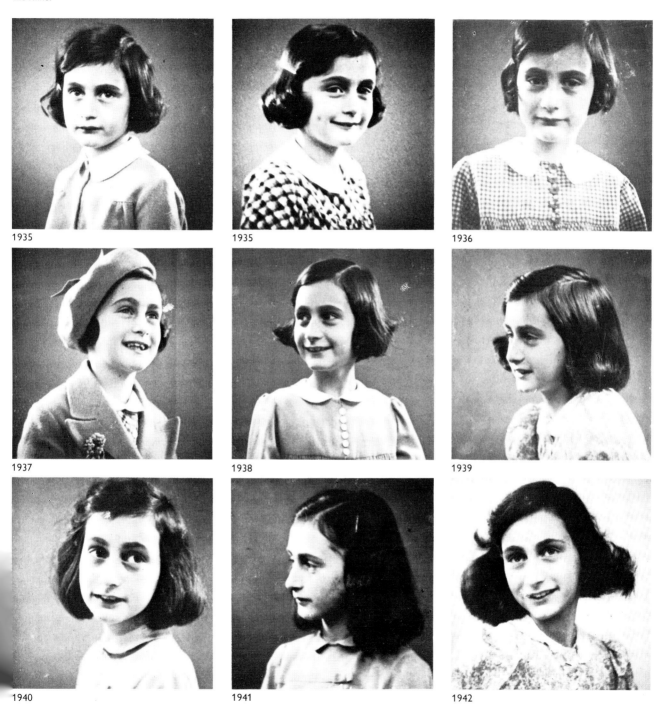

1935

1935

1936

1937

1938

1939

1940

1941

1942

In 1931 Anton Mussert establishes the National Socialist Movement (NSB). In the '30s it becomes a growing political party, and in 1935 it captures nearly 8% of the vote. The following of the NSB consists of small businessmen, civil servants and farmers who have lost faith in the country's sectarian political parties.

After 1935 the popularity of the NSB diminishes, partly because of its acknowledged anti-Semitism. When Germany invades Holland the organization still has 27,000 members.

1931 gründet Anton Mussert die 'Nationaal Socialistische Beweging' (Nationalsozialistische Bewegung, NSB). Die Partei gewinnt schnell an Zulauf und erringt 1935 knapp 8 Prozent aller Wählerstimmen. Ihre Anhänger sind vor allem Beamte, Kleinbürger und Landwirte. Nach 1935 schwindet die Popularität der NSB. Ein Grund dafür ist der immer offener zutage tretende Antisemitismus. Trotzdem zählt die NSB 1940, als deutsche Truppen die Niederlande besetzen, noch 27.000 Mitglieder.

126

128

126 Anton Mussert, leader of the NSB.
127 NSB-sympathisers.
128 NSB mass meeting.
129 The NSB is fiercely anti-communist in the election campaign: 'Mussert or Moscow'.
130 An NSB propaganda van: 'Fascism Means Action'.

126 Anton Mussert, Führer der niederländischen Nationalsozialisten.
127 NSB-Sympathisanten.
128 Massenveranstaltung der NSB.
129 In ihren Wahlkampagnen versucht die NSB vor allem antikommunistische Gefühle anzusprechen: 'Entweder Mussert oder Moskau.'
130 Propagandawagen der NSB: 'Faschismus ist Tatkraft.'

129

127

130

78

The German invasion begins on May 10, 1940 and is a complete surprise. Holland expected to remain neutral as it had done during World War I.
The occupation is swift. In a few days all important areas are seized. The prime minister and his cabinet, as well as the Royal Family, fly to England. After fierce fighting near Arnhem and the bombing of Rotterdam, Holland is forced to surrender. As of May 15, 1940, the country is under German occupation.

Der deutsche Einmarsch kommt am 10. Mai 1940 für die meisten Niederländer völlig überraschend. Man hatte darauf gehofft, wie im ersten Weltkrieg, neutral bleiben zu können. Innerhalb weniger Tage ist das ganze Land unter deutscher Kontrolle. Nach heftigen Kämpfen bei Arnheim und der Zerstörung Rotterdams kapitulieren die nationalen Streitkräfte bedingungslos. Ab dem 15. Mai 1940 sind die Niederlande deutsches Besatzungsgebiet.

132

133

131 *German paratroopers land in Holland. May 10, 1940.*
132, 133 *The bombing of Rotterdam. More than 900 people are killed; more than 24,000 houses destroyed.*
134 *Capitulation. Dutch soldiers turn in their weapons at Binnenhof, the seat of government in The Hague.*

131 *Deutsche Fallschirmspringer landen. 10. Mai 1940.*
132, 133 *Rotterdam wird angegriffen: 900 Menschen sterben bei den Bomben-Angriffen. Mehr als 24.000 Häuser werden zerstört.*
134 *Kapitulation. Auf dem 'Binnenhof' in Den Haag (dem Parlament) geben niederländische Soldaten ihre Waffen ab.*

134

80

After the first shock and terror of the military actions, most Dutch are relieved that the Germans are behaving 'properly'. The majority of Dutch do not question the right of the Germans to impose their rules. Some measures taken by the Germans, like the blackouts, seem reasonable; others seem bearable, such as the introduction of the I.D. card. Since Germany seems invincible, it stands to reason one has to adapt to the inevitable. The majority of civil servants, teachers and judges – including the Jews among them – fill out the 'Declaration of Aryanism.'

Nach der ersten Aufregung sind die meisten Niederländer erleichtert, daß sich die Besatzer so 'korrekt' verhalten. Einige der angeordneten Maßnahmen wie z.B. die Verdunklung stoßen auf Verständnis. Andere werden als gerade noch tragbar akzeptiert, wie die Einführung eines Personalausweises. Die Verweigerung jeglicher Mitarbeit steht nicht ernsthaft zur Debatte. Man arrangiert sich mit den Besatzern, da Deutschland unbesiegbar scheint.
Als die Beamten im August 1940 den 'Ariernachweis' ausfüllen sollen, tun dies fast ausnahmslos alle.

135 *Ration cards are needed to buy food.*
136 *Voting booths in Rotterdam are converted into dressing rooms for a swimming pool.*

135 *Einführung von Lebensmittelmarken.*
136 *In Rotterdam werden Stimmkabinen zu Badekabinen umgestaltet.*

135

137

137 Fences are erected alongside the Amsterdam canals because the blackout makes walking dangerous at night.

138 As of May 1941, every Dutch citizen is required to carry an identification card, a first for the Dutch. This registration takes place in Amsterdam.

137 Durch die Verdunklung ist es nachts gefährlich, an den Grachten entlang zu laufen. Deshalb werden Geländer aufgestellt.

138 Seit Mai 1941 muß jeder Niederländer einen Personalausweis bei sich tragen. Vorher gab es keine Identifikationspflicht. Registration in Amsterdam.

138

136

82

That the Germans mean business becomes clear in February 1941. The W.A., the paramilitary arm of the NSB, repeatedly enters the Jewish neighborhood of Amsterdam, displaying aggressive and brutal behavior.

Markets on the Waterloo Square and at Amstelveld are raided. The inhabitants of the Jewish neighborhood organize groups to defend their property. Heavy fighting ensues. When a W.A. man dies, the Germans retaliate. On February 22nd the Jewish neighborhood is sealed off and 400 Jewish men and boys are grabbed off the streets and from houses and coffee shops, beaten and taken away. No one knows where to.

Im Februar 1941 wird deutlich, was die Besatzer beabsichtigen. Die WA, die Wehrabteilung der NSB, tritt immer häufiger und mit zunehmender Brutalität im Amsterdamer Judenviertel auf. Die Bewohner des Judenviertels bilden Schutzgruppen, um ihr Eigentum zu verteidigen. Es kommt zu heftigen Auseinandersetzungen. Als ein WA-Mann seinen dabei erlittenen Verletzungen erliegt, greifen die Besatzer hart durch. Am 22. Februar werden alle Ausgänge des Viertels gesperrt und beinahe 400 jüdische Jungen und Männer wahllos aus Häusern und Cafés gezerrt und abtransportiert. Noch ist nicht bekannt, wohin sie kommen werden.

139, 140 *The razzia on Jonas Daniël Meijer Square. February 22, 1941.*

139, 140 *Die Razzia auf dem Jonas Daniël Meijerplein, 22. Februar 1941.*

84

To protest against this razzia, a general strike is organized immediately, primarily by the Communist Party. In and around Amsterdam tens of thousands join in a two-day strike. The occupying army retaliates with force. German troops are sent to restore order. Shots are fired. People are arrested. For fear of further reprisal, the strike is ended on February 27, 1941.

Aus Protest gegen die Razzia in Amsterdam rufen Widerstandsgruppen, insbesondere kommunistische, zu einem Generalstreik auf. Der Aufruf wird massenhaft befolgt: Am 25. und 26. Februar legen zehntausende von Arbeitern in und um Amsterdam die Arbeit nieder. Die Besatzer schlagen hart zurück: deutsche Truppenverbände werden nach Amsterdam geschickt. Auf die Demonstranten wird scharf geschossen, viele werden verhaftet. Aus Angst vor Repressalien nimmt man am 27. Februar die Arbeit wieder auf.

Wij ontvingen heden het droeve bericht, dat onze geliefde Zoon, Broeder en Kleinzoon

ARNOLD HEILBUT,

in den leeftijd van 18 jaar, in Duitschland is overleden.

Amsterdam, 2 Juli 1941.
Z. Amstellaan 89.

H. M. HEILBUT.
F. HEILBUT—CARO
en familie.

Heden ontvingen wij bericht, dat in Duitschland op 25 Juni is overleden onze innig geliefde Zoon, Broeder en Zwager

AB. LOPES DE LEAÖ LAGUNA,

in den leeftijd van 24 jaar.
Namens de familie:

B. LOPES DE LEAÖ
LAGUNA.
Verzoeke geen bezoek.
Smaragdstraat 25 I Z.

Met diep leedwezen geven wij kennis, dat onze innig geliefde eenige Zoon

PAUL JACOBUS LEO,

in den ouderdom van 27 jaar, 25 Juni in Duitschland is overleden.

I. HEIMANS JR.
J. B. HEIMANS—
VAN GELDER.
Amsterdam, 1 Juli 1941.
Watteaustraat 5.

Liever geen rouwbeklag.

142

141 Streetcar drivers on strike on Sarphati Street.
142 Several months after the razzia relatives of the arrested Jews receive death notices of their loved ones from Mauthausen concentration camp.

141 Streikende Straßenbahnfahrer in der Sarphatistraße.
142 Nur wenige Monate nach der Razzia kommen die ersten Todesnachrichten.

141

The Dutch National Socialist organizations, of which the NSB is the largest, cooperate with the Germans. Even after the razzia in February they organize mass meetings to demonstrate their anti-Semitic and pro-German attitudes. There is also collaboration based on the self-interest of people who hope to profit from the German occupation in Holland. This ranges from selling cakes to the German Army to building military installations.

Die niederländischen Nationalsozialisten arbeiten eng mit den deutschen Besatzern zusammen. Auch nach den Razzien organisieren sie noch Massenversammlungen, auf denen sie ihre antisemitische und prodeutsche Gesinnung demonstrieren. Daneben gibt es auch Kollaboration aus Eigennutz: man erhofft sich materielle Vorteile. Das reicht vom Tortenverkauf an die Wehrmacht bis zum Bunkerbau.

143 Mussert (center) and the German Reich Commissioner Seyss Inquart inspect the German troops at the Binnenhof, the seat of the government, in The Hague.
144 NSB mass meeting on Museum Square, Amsterdam. June 27, 1941.
145 1941: The windows of the New Israelitic Weekly are smashed.

143 Mussert (Mitte), Führer der NSB und Reichskommissar Seyss-Inquart (links) inspizieren die deutschen Truppen vor dem niederländischen Parlament in Den Haag.
144 27. Juni 1941. Massenkundgebung der NSB auf dem Amsterdamer Museumplein. Mussert: 'Das deutsche Volk kann auf uns zählen, wie auf seinen treuesten Hirten...'
145 1941: Die Fensterscheiben der Wochenzeitung 'Nieuw Israëlietisch Weekblad' sind zerstört.

MIT ADOLF HITLER IN EIN NEUES EUROPA!

144

143

145

The Germans appealing to deep-rooted anti-communist feelings, solicit volunteers for the war in Eastern Europe. No less than 30,000 Dutch men and boys sign up for the Waffen SS, and 17,000 are admitted beginning in April 1941. Another 15,000 volunteer for military auxiliary organizations and police groups.

Die Besatzer werben Freiwillige für den Krieg gegen die Sowjetunion. Dabei wird vor allem auf antikommunistische Gefühle gebaut. 30.000 Niederländer melden sich seit Juni 1941 freiwillig bei der Waffen-SS. 17.000 werden angemustert. Darüber hinaus bewerben sich noch 15.000 Niederländer bei militärischen Hilfsorganisationen und Polizeieinheiten wie etwa dem 'Landstorm' oder der 'Landwacht'.

146

148

149

146 *Volunteers departing for the Eastern Front in Russia. Inspection by General Seyffardt. The Hague, August 7, 1941.*
147 *Members of the NSB women's organization knit clothes for the volunteers at the Eastern Front.*
148 *Volunteers departing for the Eastern Front in Russia. The Hague, July 1941.*
149 *Mussert (left) visiting SS-volunteers at the front in Russia.*

146 *Abfahrt SS-Freiwilliger an die Ostfront, Musterung durch General Seyffardt, 7. August 1941.*
147 *Mitglieder der NSB-Frauenorganisation stricken für die Ostfrontfreiwilligen.*
148 *Abfahrt SS-Freiwilliger an die Ostfront, Juli 1941. Parole auf einem Zug: 'Weg mit Stalin, weg mit den Juden!'*
149 *Mussert (links) besucht SS-Freiwillige an der Front.*

147

90

In February 1941 the Germans force prominent Jews to form a Jewish Council, which has to represent all Jews. The Jewish leaders agree to do so in hopes of avoiding worse. The Germans use the Jewish Council as a means to execute their orders. Step by step the rights of Jews are limited, and the Jewish community is gradually isolated.

Am 12. Februar 1941 fordern die Besatzungsbehörden prominente Juden auf, einen 'Jüdischen Rat' zu bilden. Er soll fortan alle Juden vertreten. Man stimmt zu, in der Hoffnung, 'Schlimmeres verhüten' zu können. Aber die Besatzer nutzen den Rat als Instrument für die Durchsetzung ihrer Maßnahmen. Schritt für Schritt werden die Rechte der Juden eingeschränkt, die jüdische Gemeinschaft wird zunehmend isoliert.

150 *A grocery store: 'Jews not allowed'.*
151 *By February 1943 most of the shops in the Jewish ghetto are already closed.*

150 *Lebensmittelladen: 'Für Juden verboten.'*
151 *Februar 1943. Im jüdischen Viertel sind fast alle Läden geschlossen. Die meisten Juden sind deportiert oder untergetaucht.*

150

151

152

152 *Identification cards of Jews are stamped with a 'J'. Summer 1941.*
153 *A swimming pool: 'Jews not allowed'.*

152 *Sommer 1941: In die Personalausweise der Juden wird ein großes 'J' gestempelt.*
153 *Schwimmbad: 'Für Juden verboten'.*

153

155

154 Jewish teenagers at Transvaal Square, Amsterdam. Spring 1942. Many Jewish workers lived in the Transvaal quarter.
155 Jewish artists fired from their jobs advertise their availability to give concerts or performances, which are allowed in Jewish households only.
156 Amsterdam, 1942. Mr. and Mrs. Peereboom. The sign reads: 'Stars Sold Out.'

154 Jüdische Jugendliche auf dem Transvaalplatz in Amsterdam, Frühjahr 1942. In dieser Gegend lebten viele jüdische Arbeiter.
155 Jüdische Künstler, die arbeitslos werden, bieten sich für Hauskonzerte an. Sie dürfen jedoch nur bei Juden auftreten.
156 Herr und Frau Peereboom in Amsterdam, 1942. Auf dem Schild steht: 'Sterne ausverkauft'.

154

156

94

Only a tiny minority of the Dutch population actively resists the Nazis. Although most Dutchmen are anti-German or become that way once they are confronted with shortages and terror, they do not automatically choose to join the Resistance. Many factors immobilize them: fear, a fundamental rejection of civil disobedience, and religious principles based on the need to obey any government in power. But mostly the (false) choice between fascism and communism immobilizes the Dutch.

For those who do resist, political and religious differences hamper the coordination of the Resistance, especially in the first year of the occupation. There is no preparation for the occupation, let alone a tradition of resistance among the Dutch. The first acts of resistance are mostly symbolic. In 1942 and 1943 a more efficient resistance movement develops.

Nur wenige Niederländer widersetzen sich den Nazis. Dafür gibt es verschiedene Gründe: Angst, grundsätzliche Ablehnung bürgerlichen Ungehorsams, die religiös motivierte Überzeugung, daß man sich der weltlichen Macht zu fügen habe und vor allem die von den Nazis raffiniert propagierte Scheinalternative: Kommunismus oder Faschismus. Unter denen, die in den Widerstand gehen, erschweren politische und religiöse Meinungsverschiedenheiten die Zusammenarbeit. Zudem ist man auf die Besatzung schlecht vorbereitet. Erst im Laufe der Jahre 1942 und 1943 kommt es zur planmäßigen Organisation des Widerstands.

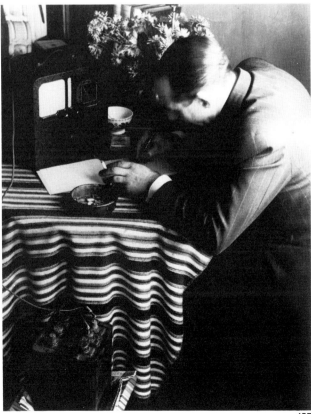

157

158

157, 158, 159 *An important activity of the Dutch resistance is the underground press. People listen to the Allied Radio stations, and the news is spread by underground stenciled or printed bulletins. About 30,000 people are involved in this activity.*

157, 158, 159 *Zu den wichtigsten Stützen des Widerstands gehören illegale Zeitungen. In ihnen erscheinen Berichte ausländischer Radiosender. An der Erstellung und dem Verteilen der Zeitungen sind rund 30.000 Niederländer beteiligt.*

159

Starting in January 1942 unemployed Jewish men are called upon to report for work in eastern Holland. Next, not only men, but entire families are summoned to go to Westerbork, a camp that serves as a collection point. From there they are deported, beginning in July 1942, to what were called 'labor camps in the East'.
The Jewish Council is pressured to deliver the required numbers for transportation to Westerbork. When the quotas are not met Jews are arrested at random. Thousands of Jews decide not to go and try to hide, although it is difficult to find a hiding place.

Seit Januar 1942 werden arbeitslose jüdische Jugendliche und Männer zur 'Arbeitsbeschaffung' ins Sammellager Westerbork eingezogen. Bald darauf werden ganze Familien nach Westerbork abtransportiert. Von dort werden sie per Zug weitergeschickt, angeblich zu 'Arbeitslagern' im Osten.
Der Jüdische Rat wird aufgefordert, die festgelegten Transportquoten für Westerbork einzuhalten.
Unterschreitungen führen zu willkürlichen Razzien. Tausende Juden folgen der Aufforderung, sich zu melden, nicht und versuchen unterzutauchen. Aber es ist schwierig, einen Unterschlupf zu finden.

160 *Where to hide? Only a few Jews can find a hiding place. Here, Jewish children hide at a farm of the Boogaard family.*
161 *During the entire month of August 1942 the razzias continue.*

160 *Untertauchen, aber wo? Nur wenige finden ein Versteck. Hier jüdische Kinder, die auf dem Land bei der Familie Boogaard untergetaucht sind.*
161 *Im gesamten Monat August 1942 kommt es zu Razzien.*

161

162 Falsification of identity papers, 1942.
163 The files from the registration office of the town of Jisp hidden from the Nazis in a barn.
164 The registration office, where vital statistics of the population are kept, is demolished by a resistance group. Amsterdam.

162 Personalausweise werden gefälscht. 1942.
163 Das Einwohnermeldeamtsbuch von Jisp verschwindet.
164 Das Einwohnermeldeamt von Amsterdam wird von einer Widerstandsgruppe in die Luft gejagt.

162

163

164

100

During 1941 the number of anti-Jewish measures increases, and the Franks start preparing to go into hiding. Thanks to the cooperation of his staff (Mr. Kraler, Mr. Koophuis, Miep Gies and Elli Vossen), Otto Frank is able to secretly prepare a hiding place for his family and the Van Daans (Mr. van Daan works with Otto Frank's company). On July 5, 1942, Margot Frank receives the notorious call to report to a 'labor camp.' The next day the Frank family moves into the 'Secret Annex.' One week later Mr. and Mrs. Van Daan and their son Peter join them, followed by Mr. Dussel.

The experiences of the people in hiding and their everyday life have been described by Anne Frank in her diary. She received this diary from her father on her 13th birthday, June 12, 1942.

Im Laufe des Jahres 1941 nehmen die anti-jüdischen Maßnahmen der Besatzer zu, und die Familie Frank beginnt mit den Vorbereitungen, unterzutauchen. Dank der Mitarbeit seiner Angestellten, Kraler, Koophuis, Miep Gies und Elli Vossen, schafft Otto Frank es, im Geheimen ein Versteck für seine Familie und die Familie van Daan vorzubereiten (Herr van Daan ist an Otto Franks Geschäft beteiligt).

Am 5. Juli 1942 erhält Margot die berüchtigte Einberufung zum 'Arbeitseinsatz', hinter der sich die Deportation in die Vernichtungslager versteckt. Schon am nächsten Tag taucht die Familie Frank unter. Eine Woche danach folgen Herr und Frau van Daan mit ihrem Sohn Peter. Ein paar Monate später kommt noch Herr Dussel hinzu. Die Geschehnisse der folgenden Jahre hat Anne in ihrem Tagebuch festgehalten. Sie hatte es zum 13. Geburtstag geschenkt bekommen.

166

165 The Annex, the hiding place.
166 The people in hiding: Otto, Edith, Anne and Margot Frank.
Mr. and Mrs. van Daan, Peter van Daan and Mr. Dussel.
167 The helpers of the people in hiding, from left to right:
Mr. Koophuis, Miep Gies, Elli Vossen and Mr. Kraler.

165 Das Hinterhaus.
166 Die Untergetauchten: Otto, Edith, Anne und Margot Frank. Herr und Frau Van Daan, Peter Van Daan und Herr Dussel.
167 Die Helfern der Unterge-tauchten. Sie bringen Essen, Kleidung und Neuigkeiten von draußen:
Mr. Koophuis, Miep Gies, Elli Vossen und Herr Koophuis.

167

168 *Anne Frank's room.* 'Our little room looked very bare at first with nothing on the walls; but thanks to Daddy who had brought my film star collection and picture postcards on beforehand, and with the aid of paste pot and brush, I have transformed the walls into one gigantic picture. This makes it look much more cheerful.' *(Anne writing in her diary, July 11, 1942).*

169 'The entrance to our hiding place has now been properly concealed. Mr. Kraler thought it would be better to put a cupboard in front of our door (because a lot of houses are being searched for hidden bicycles), but of course it had to be a movable cupboard that can open like a door. Mr. Vossen made the whole thing.' *(Anne writing in her diary on August 21, 1942.) The picture shows Mr. Koophuis next to the bookcase.*

170 *The attic of the Annex, where Anne wrote her diary most of the time.*

168 *'Unser Zimmer war mit den glatten Wänden bis jetzt noch sehr kahl; dank Vater der meine ganze Postkartensammlung und Filmstarsammlung zuvor schon mitgenommen hatte, habe ich mit Leimtopf und Pinsel die ganze Wand bestrichen und von dem Zimmer ein einziges Bild gemacht. Dadurch sieht es da viel fröhlicher aus...' Anne in ihrem Tagebuch am 11. Juli 1942.*

169 *'Unser Versteck ist nun erst ein richtiges Versteck geworden. Herr Kraler fand es nämlich besser vor unsere Zugangstür einen Schrank zu stellen, (weil viele Haussuchungen nach versteckten Fahrrädern gehalten werden.) aber dann natürlich einen Schrank der drehbar ist und der dann wie eine Tür aufgeht.' Anne in ihrem Tagebuch am 21. August 1942.*

170 *Das Dachboden des Hinterhauses. Hier schreibt Anne meistens in ihr Tagebuch.*

168

169

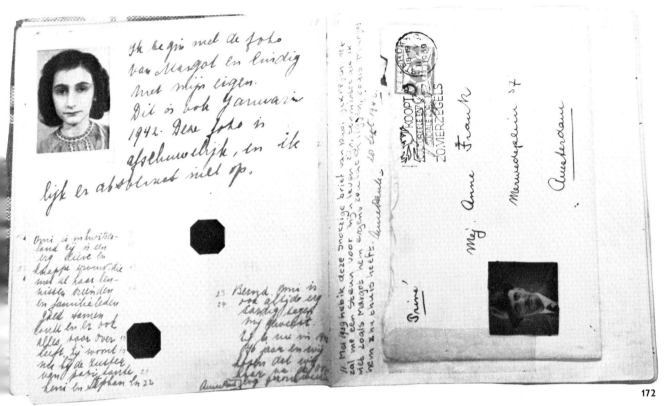

172

173

171 *View of the Prinsengracht, Westerkerk and the Annex.* 'Daddy, Mummy, and Margot can't get used to the sound of the Westertoren clock yet, which tells us the time every quarter of an hour. I can. I loved it from the start, and especially in the night it's like a faithful friend.' *(Anne writing in her diary on July 11, 1942.)*
172 *Page from Anne's first diary.*
173 'Believe me, if you have been shut up for a year and a half, it can get too much for you some days. In spite of all justice and thankfulness, you can't crush your feelings. Cycling, dancing, whistling, looking out into the world, feeling young, to know that I'm free – that's what I long for; still, I mustn't show it, because I sometimes think if all eight of us begin to pity ourselves, or went about with discontented faces, where would it lead us?' *(Anne writing in her diary, December 24, 1943)*

171 'Vater, Mutter und Margot können sich noch immer nicht an das Geräusch der Westerturmglocke gewöhnen, die jede Viertelstunde sagt wie spät es ist. Ich schon, ich fand es sofort schön und vor allem nachts ist es so etwas Vertrautes.' Anne in ihrem Tagebuch am 11. Juli 1942.
172 *Seite aus Annes erstem Tagebuch.*
173 'Glaub mir, wenn man 1½ Jahre eingeschlossen sitzt, dann kann es einem an manchen Tagen mal zuviel werden. Aller Berechtigung oder Undankbarkeit zum Trotz; Gefühle lassen sich nicht wegschieben. Radfahren, tanzen, pfeifen, die Welt sehen, mich jung fühlen, wissen daß ich frei bin, danach sehne ich mich und doch darf ich es nicht zeigen, denn stell dir vor wenn wir alle 8 anfingen uns zu beklagen oder unzufriedene Gesichter zu machen, wohin soll das führen?' *(Freitag, 24. Dezember, 1943)*

60 TIGHTENING OF THE REPRESSION AND RESISTANCE

60 UNTERDRÜCKUNG UND WIDERSTAND VERSCHÄRFEN SICH

In the autumn of 1942 the German military loses ground. Allied advances in North Africa, the Soviet counterattack and the fall of Mussolini stimulate the Resistance. But simultaneously repression for the remaining Dutchmen is increased.

In September 1944 among the non-Jewish population 250,000 are in hiding; 12,500 are prisoners of war; 7,000, political prisoners; and 300,000, forced laborers. Aside from those groups, about 900,000 people are forced to leave their homes and move. The total population in Holland then is about nine million. Starting in the summer of 1944, many resistance fighters are summarily shot. Hundreds of others are executed in retaliation for acts of resistance.

Ende 1942 kommt der Vormarsch der deutschen Wehrmacht zum stehen. Die Eroberung von Teilen Nordafrikas durch die alliierten Truppen, die erfolgreiche sowjetische Gegenoffensive, sowie der Sturz Mussolinis ermutigen den Widerstand. Die Aktionen nehmen zu. Zugleich wird der Terror gegen die noch übriggebliebene Bevölkerung verschärft. Im September 1944 befinden sich unter der nicht-jüdischen Bevölkerung von ca. 9 Mio. Niederländern 250.000 Untergetauchte, 12.500 Kriegsgefangene, 7.000 politische Häftlinge und 300.000 Zwangsarbeiter. Etwa 900.000 Menschen werden gezwungen, ihre Häuser zu verlassen und umzuziehen.

175

176

174 The liquidation of a traitor.
Resistance groups have emotional
discussions whether one has the right
to execute traitors.
175 In 1943 and 1944 tens of
thousands of men are sent to
Germany to work.
176 Many men and young adults go
into hiding, mostly on farms, to
escape being forced to work in
Germany.

174 Liquidierung eines Verräters.
Innerhalb der Widerstandsbewegung
sind die Meinungsunterschiede groß,
ob man einen Verräter überhaupt
liquidieren darf.
175 Zehntausende Niederländer
werden 1943 und 1944 zum Arbeitseinsatz nach Deutschland verschleppt.
176 Viele versuchen, sich dem
Arbeitseinsatz in Deutschland durch
die Flucht aufs Land zu entziehen.

177 During a football match the German police arrest men and send them to work in Germany. February 1944.
178 Executed resistance fighters.
179 In September 1944 the Dutch Railway workers go on strike. German trains are attacked by sabotage groups.

177 Razzia während eines Fußballspiels. Männer werden wahllos aufgegriffen und zum Arbeitseinsatz in Deutschland gezwungen. Eindhoven, Februar 1944.
178 Hingerichtete Widerstandskämpfer.
179 September 1944: Das Personal der niederländischen Eisenbahn streikt. Züge nach und aus Deutschland werden mit Anschlägen und Sabotage gestoppt.

177

178

110

Most razzias and transportations to the camps occur at night. In Amsterdam most Jews are first brought to the Jewish Theater and then on to Westerbork. The majority stay there several weeks, some more than a year.

In 1943 one transport follows another until the camp is full and life becomes unbearable. Westerbork, however, is not a final destination. Rather, it is a collection point to transport the Jews to the extermination camps.

Die meisten Razzien und Abtransporte finden abends statt. In Amsterdam werden die Juden erst zum 'Jüdischen Theater' gebracht und von dort aus nach Westerbork an der deutschen Grenze. Hier bleiben die Deportierten zumeist einige Wochen, manche aber auch länger als ein Jahr. Im Laufe des Jahres 1943 nimmt die Zahl der Transporte enorm zu, und das Lager ist ständig überfüllt. Aber Westerbork ist nur ein Durchgangslager auf dem Weg zu den Vernichtungslagern im Osten.

180

180 *Waiting for the departure to Westerbork. Amsterdam, May 26, 1943. The photographs were taken for an SS-magazine.*
181 *Departure from Amsterdam's Muiderpoort Station to Westerbork.*
182 *Westerbork, the Dutch transit camp.*

180 *Amsterdam: Sammlung zum Transport nach Westerbork. Diese Fotos vom 26. Mai 1943 wurden im Auftrag einer SS-Zeitschrift gemacht.*
181 *Abfahrt von Amsterdam nach Westerbork.*
182 *Durchgangslager Westerbork.*

62, 63 ENDLÖSUNG ('THE FINAL SOLUTION')

62, 63 ENDLÖSUNG

112

When Germany marches through Eastern Europe, the army is followed by SS special units (Einsatzgruppen) that start the mass execution of Jews. More than one million Jews are shot. In 1941 the decision is made 'to make Europe clean of Jews.' During the Wannsee Conference in January 1942 plans are made to annihilate the 11 million European Jews.
The plans become known as the Endlösung, the 'Final Solution of the Jewish Question'. Extermination and labor camps are built. A large number of the deported Jews – mostly the elderly, mothers and children – are gassed upon arrival. The others must work a couple of months until they die of exhaustion. In this way nearly six million Jews are killed. In addition to the Jews, countless others die in concentration camps: political opponents, homosexuals, Jehovah's Witnesses, 'anti-social elements', Russian prisoners of war and at least 220,000 gypsies.

Den deutschen Truppenverbänden in Ost-Europa folgen sogenannte 'Einsatzgruppen': SS, die mit der Ausrottung der Juden beginnt. Bei Massenexekutionen werden mehr als eine Million Juden erschossen. 1942: Auf der 'Wannseekonferenz' planen führende Nazis die 'Endlösung der Judenfrage' – die systematische Ausrottung von 11 Millionen europäischer Juden. Hierfür werden spezielle Vernichtungslager errichtet. Während Mütter mit Kindern sowie alte Menschen aussortiert und in die Gaskammern getrieben werden, werden alle 'Arbeitsfähigen' in Baracken zusammengepfercht und von morgens bis abends zu Schwerstarbeit eingesetzt. Die meisten sterben an Unterernährung, Erschöpfung, fallen Krankheiten zum Opfer. Auf diese Weise werden etwa 6 Millionen Juden in den Konzentrationslagern umgebracht. Darüberhinaus sterben zahllose andere Opfer der Nazis in den Lagern: politische Gegner, Homosexuelle, Zeugen Jehovas, sogenannte 'Asoziale', russische Kriegsgefangene und mindestens 220.000 Roma und Sinti.

183 *Dutch Jews departing from Westerbork for Auschwitz.*
184 *Jews in Eastern Europe are rounded up by special command groups ('Einsatzgruppen') and murdered.*

183 *Niederländische Juden auf dem Weg von Westerbork nach Auschwitz.*
184 *Osteuropäische Juden werden von 'Einsatzgruppen' zusammengetrieben und ermordet.*

184

185

186

185 Upon arrival in Auschwitz Jews are divided into two groups: those who can still work and those who are to be exterminated immediately.
186 The IG Farben Co. operates an enormous factory near Auschwitz. The death toll among the forced laborers at this site is extremely high.
187 Those not immediately killed have a number tatooed on their arm. This gypsy woman is one of the few survivors.
188 Guards at Dachau.

185 Bei der Ankunft im Vernichtungslager Auschwitz wird sofort selektiert. Kinder, Kranke und alte Menschen werden gleich vergast. Die anderen müssen bis zum Tode arbeiten.
186 Die Firma I.G.-Farben hat eine Fabrik in der Nähe des Lagers, in der Gefangene arbeiten. Die Sterbequoten sind erschreckend hoch.
187 Jeder, der bei der Ankunft nicht sofort vergast wird, bekommt eine Nummer eintätowiert. Diese Sintifrau gehört zu den wenigen Überlebenden.
188 Aufseher im KZ Dachau.

187

188

On August 4, 1944, the German police make a raid on the 'Secret Annex.' All the occupants are arrested and sent to concentration camps.

Am 4. August fällt die 'Grüne Polizei' ins Hinterhaus ein, verhaftet alle Versteckten und schickt sie über Westerbork nach Auschwitz.

189

189 *The train from Westerbork to Auschwitz.*
190 *A list of deportees on the last train from Westerbork to Auschwitz contains the names of the Frank family. Mrs. Edith Frank-Holländer is killed by the hardships of Auschwitz. Mr. Van Daan dies in the gaschamber. Peter van Daan is taken by the SS when the concentration camp was abandoned because of the approach of the Russian army. He dies in Mauthausen. Mr. Dussel dies in the Neuengamme concentration camp.*

At the end of October Margot and Anne are transported back into Germany, to Bergen-Belsen. Both of them contract typhus. They die in March 1945. Mrs. van Daan also dies in Bergen-Belsen. Otto Frank is liberated by the Russian troops at Auschwitz.

189 *Der Zug von Westerbork nach Auschwitz.*
190 *Die Transportliste des letzten Zuges, der von Westerbork nach Auschwitz fuhr. Auf der Liste stehen die Namen der Familie Frank. Am 4. August fällt die 'Grüne Polizei' ins Hinterhaus ein, verhaftet alle Versteckten und schickt sie über Westerbork nach Auschwitz. Frau Edith Frank-Holländer stirbt im Konzentrationslager Auschwitz an den Entbehrungen. Herr van Daan wird vergast. Peter wird von der SS mitgeführt, als das Lager wegen der aufrückenden russischen Truppen*

geräumt wird. Er stirbt später in Mauthausen. Herr Dussel stirbt im Lager Neuengamme. Anne und Margot werden im Oktober des Jahres 1944 ins Lager Bergen-Belsen gebracht. Dort verbringen sie den Winter. Doch sie infizieren sich beide mit Typhus und sterben kurz hintereinander im März 1945. Im gleichen Lager stirbt auch Frau van Daan. Als einziger Überlebender der Untergetauchten erlebt Otto Frank die Befreiung des Lagers Auschwitz durch die Russen.

JUDENTRANSPORT AUS DEN NIEDERLANDEN - LAGER WESTERBORK

Haeftlinge

301. ✓Engers	Isidor — ✓30.4. 93 —	Kaufmann
302 ✓ Engers	Leonard	15.6. 20 —	Lamdarbeiter
303 ✓ Franco	Manfred — ✓1.5. 05 —	Verleger
304. Frank	Arthur	22.8. 81	Kaufmann
305. Frank ×	Isaac	✓29.11.87	Installateur
306. Frank	Margot	16.2. 26	ohne
307. Frank ✓	Otto	✓12.5. 89	Kaufmann
308. ✓ Frank-Hollaender	Edith	16.1. 00	ohne
309. Frank	Anneliese	12.6. 29	ohne
310. v.Franck	Sara —	27.4. 02 —	Typistin
311. Franken	Rozanna	16.5. 96 —	Landarbeiter
312. ✓ Franken-Weyand	Johanna	24.12.96 ✓	Landbauer
313. Franken	Hermann — ✓12.5.34	ohne
314. Franken	Louis	10.8. 17 —	Gaertner
315. Franken R	Rosalina	29.3. 27	Landbau
316. Frankfort	Alex	14.11.19 —	Dr.i.d.Oekonomie
317. Frankfort-Elsas	Regina	11.12.19	Apoth-.Ass.
318. Frankfoort ×	Elias	✓22.10.98 —	Schneider
319. ✓Frankfort R	Max	20.6. 21	Schneider
320. ✓Frankfort-Weijl R	Hetty	29.3. 24	Naeherin
321. ✓Frankfort-Werkendam R Rosette	24.6.98	Schriftstellerin
322. ✓Frijda	Hermann	22.6. 87 —	Hochschullehrer
323. Frenk	Henriette	28.4. 21	Typistin
324. Frenk R	Rosa	15.3.24	Haushalthilfe
325. Friezer	Isaac	10.3. 20 —	Korrespondent
326. ✓ Fruitman-Vlessche-			
dráger R Fanny	24.1. 03	ohne
327. Gans ×	Elie	✓24.10.03 —	Betriebleiter
328. Gans-Koopman R	Gesina	20.12.05	Maschinestrickerin
329. Gans	Kalman —	6.3. 79	Diamantarbeiter
330. Gans R	Klara	12.5. 13	Naeherin
331. Gans ·	Paul —	27.9. 08 —	Landbauer
332. v.Gelder	Abraham —	9.11.78	Metzger
333. v.Gelder-de Jong	Reintje	22.10.81	ohne
334. v.Gelder	Alexander	27.6. 03 —	Kaufmann

65 D-DAY AND THE LIBERATION OF SOUTHERN HOLLAND

65 'D-DAY', 'DOLLER DIENSTAG' UND DIE BEFREIUNG DER SÜD-NIEDERLANDE

In 1944 the Allied Forces gain momentum in Europe. The Germans retreat from Eastern Europe. The liberation of Western Europe begins with D-Day. In one day, June 6, 1944, 156,000 Allied soldiers land in northern France.

Following the successful invasion, rumors about the liberation begin. In Holland on September 5, 1944, known as 'Wild Tuesday,' most people believe the liberation is near. Southern Holland is, in reality, liberated.

1944 werden die Deutschen an allen Fronten zurückgeschlagen. In Osteuropa rücken die sowjetischen Truppen rasch vor, und in Westeuropa landen am 6. Juni 1944 156.000 alliierte Soldaten in der Normandie. In den Niederlanden kommen Gerüchte auf, die Befreiung stehe unmittelbar bevor. Nicht zuletzt aufgrund allzu optimistischer englischer Rundfunkberichte glauben viele Menschen, der Krieg sei so gut wie vorbei. Am 5. September 1944 kommt es zum 'Dollen Dienstag': Es hagelt Spott und Prügel für Kollaborateure und Besatzer. Wenig später wird der Süden des Landes tatsächlich befreit.

Dann aber kommt der alliierte Vormarsch zum stehen.

191

192

193

191 D-Day (Decision-Day): American
and British troops land in Normandy,
France. June 6, 1944.
192 September 5, 1944, known as
'Wild Tuesday'. NSB members hurry
to leave Holland. The Hague Railway
station.
193 'Wild Tuesday': The village of
Rijswijk waits in vain for the Allied
troops to come.
194 Allied soldiers hand out chewing
gum in the liberated south of Holland.

191 D-Day (Decision Day, Tag der Ent-
scheidung): Landung amerikanischer
und englischer Truppen an der nord-
französischen Küste, 6. Juni 1944.
192 Die Bevölkerung Rijswijks wartet
am 'Dollen Dienstag' vergeblich auf
die alliierten Befreier.
193 'Doller Dienstag', 5. September
1944. Flüchtende NSB-Männer auf
dem Bahnhof von Den Haag.
194 Alliierte Soldaten verteilen im
Süden des Landes Kaugummi.

194

120

The Dutch Railway halts service in September 1944 because of a railway strike ordered by the Dutch government in exile in London. As a result, the Germans retaliate by forbidding food to be brought to the cities. An enormous shortage follows, worsened by food confiscations by the Germans. When coal and other fuel are not delivered to the cities, the situation becomes critical. Everything that can burn is used for heat. Everything edible is eaten, even tulip bulbs. Thousands of children are sent to the countryside to be fed. About 22,000 people die of hunger. Tens of thousands are seriously ill. Meanwhile, the Germans take anything of value to Germany: bicycles, machines, factory equipment, streetcars and cattle, for example.

September 1944: die Eisenbahner streiken, nachdem die niederländische Exilregierung in London dazu aufgerufen hat. Zur Strafe stoppen die Besatzer alle Lebensmitteltransporte in die großen Städte. Was dennoch ankommt, wird beschlagnahmt. Als schließlich auch keine Brennstoffe mehr geliefert werden, wird die Lage besonders kritisch. Alles Brennbare wird verheizt, alles Eßbare verschlungen: sogar Tulpenzwiebeln kommen auf den Teller. Tausende von Kindern werden auf dem Land untergebracht. In diesem Winter sterben 22.000 Menschen vor Hunger. Die Besatzer schleppen alles ab, was ihnen wertvoll erscheint: Maschinen, Straßenbahnwagen, Vieh, Fahrräder usw.

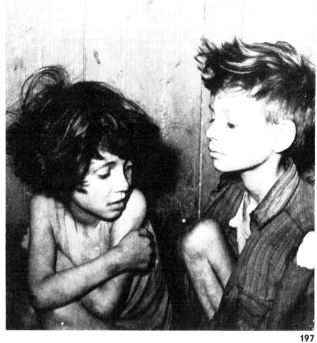

196

197

195 Children remove an old door for firewood.
196 People burn wood from their own houses for fuel.
197 Hungry children.
198 In the countryside thousands of people try to exchange goods for food.

195 Kinder sammeln Holz.
196 Sogar das Holz der eigenen Wohnung muß zum Heizen herhalten.
197 Hungernde Kinder.
198 Tausende ziehen aufs Land und versuchen Wertgegenstände gegen Nahrung zu tauschen.

198

122

In April 1945 British planes drop food over starving Holland, allowing many thousands to survive. The announcement is made over British radio.

A few weeks later the war is over. The remainder of Holland is liberated by the Allied Forces. Festivities are organized throughout the country. At the same time the Nazis and their collaborators are arrested. Over 75% of the Dutch Jews – more than 100,000 people – are killed during the war. Of 24,000 Jews who found a hiding place, 16,000 survive.

Die britische Luftwaffe wirft Ende April 1945 Nahrungspakete über Holland ab. Die Aktionen werden über die englischen Sender angekündigt und sind sehr willkommen: Tausende überleben so den Krieg, der schon wenige Wochen später beendet ist. Am 5. Mai 1945 werden die letzten Teile der Niederlande befreit. Im ganzen Land feiert man das Ende der deutschen Besatzung. NSB-Anhänger und Kollaborateure werden verhaftet. 75% der niederländischen Juden überlebt den Krieg nicht. Mehr als 100.000 Menschen werden ermordet. Von 24.000 untergetauchten Juden erleben 16.000 die Befreiung.

199 British bombers loaded with
parcels of food above Rotterdam.
April 30, 1945.
200 Liberation festivities in
Amsterdam's Red Light District.

199 Britische Bomber mit Nahrungs-
paketen über Rotterdam, 30.4.1945.
200 Das Vergnügungsviertel in
Amsterdam. Die Befreiung wird
gefeiert.

123

On May 8, 1945, the German Army surrenders unconditionally. During the last months of the war German cities are so heavily bombed that little remains. Hitler and Goebbels commit suicide. Many Nazis are arrested. The Soviet, American and other Allied troops work closely to defeat Nazi Germany.
Although the liberation comes too late for millions, many in prisons and concentration camps can be saved.
Germany is brought under joint Allied authority.

Am 8. Mai kapituliert das deutsche Heer bedingungslos. Nach schweren Bombardements der vorangegangenen Monate liegen große Teile der deutschen Städte in Schutt und Asche. Hitler und Goebbels begehen in Berlin Selbstmord. Viele Nazis werden verhaftet. Bei der Eroberung Deutschlands arbeiten die USA, England, Frankreich und die Sowjetunion eng zusammen. Obwohl die Hilfe für Millionen zu spät kommt, können viele aus Gefängnissen und Konzentrationslagern befreit werden. Bis auf weiteres wird Deutschland alliiertes Besatzungsgebiet.

201

201 In the German countryside Americans say hello to Russians.
202 Soviet and US-troops meet at the Elbe river in Germany.
203 Frankfurt.
204 Jewish survivors, liberated from Theresiënstadt, return to Frankfurt.
205 Some very young boys, members of the 'Volkssturm', are among the arrested soldiers.

201 Irgendwo in Deutschland: Amerikaner grüßen Russen.
202 Sowjetische und amerikanische Truppen treffen sich an der Elbe.
203 Das zerstörte Frankfurt.
204 Jüdische Überlebende des KZ Theresienstadt kehren nach Frankfurt zurück.
205 'Das letzte Aufgebot des Führers': die Hitlerjugend.

203

125

204

202

205

69 LIBERATION OF THE CONCENTRATION CAMPS

The Allied advance into Germany influences the situation at the concentration camps. In January 1945 the Nazis clear the camps by forcing prisoners to walk hundreds of miles through snow and rain. Thousands die.

What the Allied Forces find when they finally arrive at the concentration camps is indescribable. For the survivors, a difficult journey home begins. For many of them the homecoming is a bitter disappointment. Most have lost friends and family. Houses are occupied. Property is stolen. Many survivors encounter disbelief and ignorance about their experiences in the camps. Only 4,700 Jewish survivors return to Holland from the camps.

69 DIE BEFREIUNG DER KONZENTRATIONS-LAGER UND HEIMKEHR DER HÄFTLINGE

Als sich die alliierten Truppen den Lagern nähern, werden diese geräumt. Oft werden die Häftlinge gezwungen, mit den abrückenden Wachmannschaften mitzuziehen. Tausende sterben auf diesen Todesmärschen durch Schnee und Regen. Die Alliierten finden grauenhafte Verhältnisse vor, als sie die Lager befreien. Für die Überlebenden beginnt nun eine schwierige Heimreise. Die Heimkehr endet häufig mit einer bitteren Enttäuschung: Familie und Freunde sind umgekommen, der Besitz ist geraubt. Die Zurückgebliebenen können zudem das Ausmaß der Leiden, die die Häftlinge erfahren haben, nicht ermessen und begreifen.

Nur 4.700 Juden kehren aus den Konzentrations- und Vernichtungslagern in die Niederlande zurück.

207

206 The liberation of Dachau.
207 After the liberation of Bergen-Belsen, the camp where Anne and Margot Frank died, the barracks are set afire to radically desinfect the places of contamination with typhoid fever.
208 Temporary repatriation camps are set up in hotels and schools.

206 Die Befreiung Dachaus.
207 Im befreiten Bergen-Belsen – hier starben Anne und Margot Frank – werden die Baracken wegen der bestehenden Typhusgefahr niederge-brannt.
208 Für die Überlebenden werden in Hotels, Schulen und anderen Unter-künften Auffanglager eingerichtet.

208

The first photographs of the concentration camps cause a tremendous shock everywhere – how could a thing like this happen?
Twenty-two of the most important Nazi leaders are tried by the International Tribunal in Nuremberg in 1946. New legal principles are drafted there to prevent similar atrocities in the future. Another important document is the 'Universal Declaration of Human Rights,' adopted in 1948 by the United Nations, which was founded in 1945.

Die ersten Fotos aus den Konzentrationslagern verursachen auf der ganzen Welt einen Schock: wie konnte so etwas um Gottes Willen geschehen? 22 der wichtigsten Führungsmänner der Nazis stehen 1946 vor einem internationalen Tribunal in Nürnberg vor Gericht. Es entstehen Rechtsnormen, die eine Wiederholung der Naziverbrechen unmöglich machen sollen. Ein wichtiges Dokument ist die 'Erklärung der Menschenrechte', die 1948 von den 1945 gegründeten 'Vereinten Nationen' verabschiedet wird.

209 *During the International Tribunal. Nuremberg, 1946.*
210 *Bergen-Belsen.*

209 *Während der Nürnberger Prozesse, 1946.*
210 *Bergen-Belsen.*

129

71 THE PUBLICATION OF ANNE FRANK'S DIARY

71 DIE VERÖFFENTLICHUNG DES TAGESBUCHES VON ANNE FRANK

Upon his return to Amsterdam, Otto Frank realizes he is the only survivor of his family. Soon thereafter, Miep Gies gives Anne's papers and writings to him. After the people in hiding had been taken away, the helpers returned to the Annex and took as much as possible before the Annex was cleared. Miep had kept Anne's papers during that time. Friends persuade Otto Frank to publish Anne's diary. 'The Diary of Anne Frank' appears in 1947 under the title 'Het Achterhuis' (The Annex). To date, more than 50 different editions have appeared, and more than 20 million copies have been sold. The house where Anne and the others lived in hiding is now a museum, operated by the Anne Frank Foundation, which was founded in 1957. Apart from the preservation of the Annex, the Foundation tries to stimulate the fight against anti-Semitism, racism and fascism with information and educational projects.

Als Otto Frank nach Amsterdam zurückkehrt, wird ihm deutlich, daß er der einzige Überlebende der Familie ist. Schon nach kurzer Zeit überreicht Miep Gies ihm Annes Tagebücher, die sie vor der Räumung des Hauses in Sicherheit gebracht hatte. Auf Anraten von Freunden beschließt Otto Frank, Annes Tagebuch zu veröffentlichen. 1947 erscheint die erste Auflage unter dem Titel 'Het Achterhuis' (Das Hinterhaus). Seither ist das Tagebuch in mehr als 50 Sprachen übersetzt und 20 millionenmal gedruckt worden.
Seit 1957 ist das Anne Frank Haus ein Museum, das von der Anne Frank Stiftung verwaltet wird. Daneben beschäftigt sich die Stiftung auch mit Bildungsarbeit und dem Erstellen von Unterrichtsmaterialien.

211 *Otto Frank remarries in Amsterdam. His new wife is Elfriede Markovits. November 10, 1953. He dies in August 1980, at the age of 91.*
212 *Advertisement from the Dutch newspaper 'Het Vrije Volk' (The Free People). August 1, 1945. Otto Frank is looking for his daughters Margot and Anne.*
213 *Miep Gies (left) and her husband Jan show British schoolchildren from Manchester the hiding-place of the Frank family. The children were prizewinners of a drawing competition about discrimination. May 1987.*
214 *Cover of the first Dutch edition of Anne's diary.*

INLICHTINGEN GEVRAAGD OMTRENT

10 Juni '44 naar Amersfoort tot Oct. '44 en vermoedelijk naar Buchenwalde of Neuengamme vervoerd. A. BOSCH, Soembawastr. 49 hs. of mevr. L. GERRITSEN—STRAALMAN, Jan Steenstr. 27, Deventer.
LOUIS VOORSANGER, geb. 5-12-'85, vertrokk. Westerbork 18 Mei '43 n. Duitsland. E. Auerhaan, Pieter Aertszstr. 119 III.
IRMA SPIELMANN, geb. 10-4-'94 Wenen, Tsj. Slow. nation. Weggevoerd Westerborg 23-3-'43. Wie weet iets van dit transport? Spielmann, Scheldestr. 181 III, Zuid.
MARGOT FRANK (19 j.) en **ANNA FRANK** (16 j.), in Jan. op transp. vanuit Bergen-Belzen. O. Frank, Prinsengracht 263, tel. 37059.
Mijn man **ALFRED v. GELDEREN**. (Oct. 1942 uit Westerb.) en kinderen **DORA ROSA en FREDERIK MARTHIJN** (24-7-1942 uit Westerb.) Marianne v. Gelderen—Engelander, Jozef Israëlkade 126 II.
FRANCISCUS JOHANNES MAAS geb. 19-10-'23, werkz. bij Machinefabriek Winger en Co. Waltersdorf Kreis Zittau Saksen Duitsland. Inl. gevr. van hen, die hem na 16 Sept. 1944 hebben gezien. J. Ch.

212

ANNE FRANK

Het Achterhuis

DAGBOEKBRIEVEN
VAN 14 JUNI 1942 - 1 AUGUSTUS 1944

214

211 Am 10. November 1953 heiratet Otto Frank in zweiter Ehe Elfriede Markowitz, Amsterdam. Otto Frank stirbt im Alter von 91 Jahren im August 1980.
212 Anzeige aus der niederländischen Zeitung 'Het Vrije Volk' (Das Freie Volk) vom 1. August 1945. Otto Frank sucht nach seinen Töchtern Margot und Anne.
213 Miep Gies (links) und ihr Mann Jan zeigen das Hinterhaus englischen Kindern aus Manchester, die einen Malwettbewerb über Diskriminierung gewonnen haben. Mai 1987.
214 Umschlag der ersten niederländischen Ausgabe von Anne Franks Tagebuch.

213

132

The systematic murder of millions of Jews and others is an unprecedented crime in the history of mankind. More than forty years after the liberation, however, the question asked more often is, whether this period still deserves so much attention. 'We have now remembered enough ... One should forgive and forget', can be heard.

The Anne Frank Centre finds it necessary to inform younger generations about the period 1933-1945, and states that remembering can help to prevent it ever to happen again.

In Germany and Austria a tendency can be found to equalize all the dead from the Secon World War – Waffen-SS soldiers and victims of Allied bombings, as well as victims of the concentration camps.

In the countries that were occupied by the Nazis the collaboration is often a forgotten chapter in the history books. The same goes for the indifference toward the persecution of Jews, gypsies, homosexuals and others. A general problem arises with comparisons between Nazi crimes and any other form of oppression and mass murder. The word 'Holocaust' is often used for anything with which one does not agree. The danger is that in this way the Shoah is reduced to just another black page from history.

Der systematische Mord an Millionen Juden und anderen ist ein unübertroffener Tiefpunkt der Geschichte. Gut vierzig Jahre nach der Befreiung wird immer häufiger die Frage gestellt, ob man dieser Zeit noch immer so viel Aufmerksamkeit schenken sollte. 'Es muß endlich Schluß sein', 'wir müssen endlich vergessen und vergeben', so hört man.

Die Anne Frank Stiftung ist der Ansicht, daß es notwendig bleibt, jüngere Generationen über die Zeit zwischen 1933 und 1945 zu informieren. Gedenken trägt dazu bei, daß sich etwas ähnliches nicht wiederholen kann.

In Deutschland und Österreich sind Tendenzen spürbar, alle Toten des Zweiten Weltkrieges – Bombenopfer und Soldaten der Waffen-SS, wie Opfer von Verfolgung und Widerstand – über einen Kamm zu scheren.

Ein allgemeines Problem ist das Vergleichen der Nazi-Verbrechen mit allerlei anderen Formen von Unterdrückung und Massenmord. Das gleiche gilt für den Begriff 'Holocaust'. Die Gefahr entsteht, daß die Shoah zu einem schwarzen Kapitel unter vielen wird.

215 The first monument to commemorate the murder of thousands of homosexuals by the Nazis, was built in Amsterdam, 1987.
216 During the commemoration of the 40th anniversary of the liberation, chancellor Kohl (left) and president Reagan (second from right) pay a controversial visit to both the concentration camp Bergen-Belsen and a cemetery of soldiers in Bitburg. May 1985.
217 Demonstrators against Reagans visit to Bitburg. The equation of SS men and concentration camp victims arouses international protests. 'Why, Mr. President, are you visiting a cemetery where members of the SS are buried?'
218 Often activists try to add weigh to their argument by comparing the case they fight with the Holocaust. Here the anti-abortion movement in the United States. 'Abortion – Auschwitz. The American Holocaust'.

215

216

217

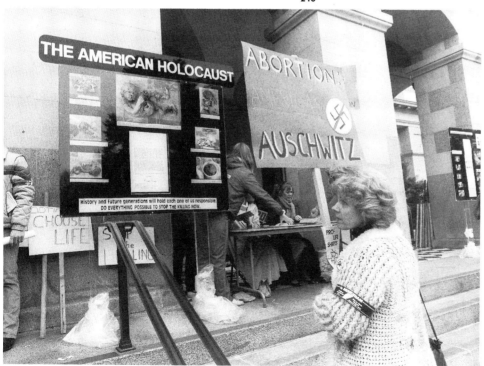

218

215 Das erste Monument zum Gedenken an die Ermordung tausender Homosexueller durch die Nazis steht seit 1987 in Amsterdam, in der Nähe des Anne Frank Hauses.
216 Im Rahmen der Gedenkfeiern zum 40. Jahrestag der Befreiung vom Faschismus besuchen Bundeskanzler Kohl (links) und Präsident Ronald Reagan (zweiter von rechts) das Konzentrationslager Bergen-Belsen und den Soldatenfriedhof in Bitburg, was zu Kontroversen führt. Mai 1985.
217 Demonstration gegen den Reagan-Besuch in Bitburg. Die Gleichsetzung von SS-Leuten und den Opfern der Konzentrationslager führt zu internationalen Protesten. 'Herr Präsident, warum besuchen Sie einen Friedhof, auf dem Mitglieder der SS begraben sind?'
218 Oft wird versucht, den Holocaust für politische Ziele zu gebrauchen. Hier eine Bewegung gegen Abtreibung in den Vereinigten Staaten.
'Abtreibung – Auschwitz. Der amerikanische Holocaust'.

73 NEO-NAZI'S AND THE DENIAL OF THE HOLOCAUST

73 NEONAZIS UND DIE VERLEUGNUNG DES 'HOLOCAUST'

There are still small groups denying the Nazi's mass murders. They call the Nazi crimes 'The hoax of the 20th century', and in this way try to rehabilitate and excuse National Socialism.

Immer noch gibt es kleine Gruppen, die den Massenmord durch die Nationalsozialisten abstreiten. Sie nennen diese Verbrechen 'den Betrug des Jahrhunderts'. Auf diese Weise versuchen sie, den Nationalsozialismus zu verharmlosen.

219 *The defaced barrack of the former Flossenbürg concentration camp, April 1983: 'Wiesenthal is a Jewish liar, down with the concentration camp lies.'*

219 *Parole auf einer Baracke im ehemaligen Konzentrationslager Flossenbürg. April 1983.*

220 *Neo-Nazi publication by Richard Verrall of the National Front: "Holocaust story an evil hoax." London, 1987.*

220 *Neonazistische Publikation 'Holocaust News', herausgegeben von Richard Verrall, Mitglied der 'National Front': "Die Geschichte der Holocaust, eine teuflische Erfindung." London, 1987.*

'Holocaust' News

No.1   PUBLISHED BY THE CENTRE FOR HISTORICAL REVIEW   15p

'HOLOCAUST' STORY AN EVIL HOAX

DO YOU BELIEVE that six million Jews were systematically exterminated by the Nazis in gas chambers during the Second World War? Do you consider it shocking that anyone could bring themselves to question the truth of the 'Holocaust' story?

If you answer "Yes" to these questions, then you will not find reading *'Holocaust' News* a comforting and reassuring experience.

But if you possess the courage to pursue the truth, then you will read on.

One of the first facts to disturb you is that there is an increasing number of people world-wide who reject the 'Holocaust' story as an absurd propaganda myth.

PERSECUTION

These people *(see page 2)* are not "neo-Nazi fanatics" or "anti-Jewish bigots". They include reputable academics attached to university history, philosophy, engineering and law faculties, as well as prominent writers, lawyers, diplomats and civil rights campaigners.

Among their number may be counted Jews, radical Socialists, Jehovah's Witnesses and indeed former camp inmates! None of these people have any reason to be pro-Nazi.

All of them are today being subjected in varying degrees to relentless book-burning persecution because their researches have blown irreparable holes in the 'Holocaust' story.

The identity of those who are persecuting these courageous "Historical Revisionists" — and why — is all tied up with the identity of the people who invented and propagated the 'Holocaust' myth in the first place — and why.

Clearly the second obstacle – world public opinion – had to be dealt with before the first obstacle – the Palestinians – could be cleared out of the way.

It is one of history's ironies that the opportunity for the Zionist land-grabbers to solve their public relations problem was presented to them by their arch-enemy, Adolf Hitler.

When the Second World War broke out Hitler considered that the Jews were largely to blame for it, and so began an extensive programme of resettlement and internment as did Roosevelt to Japanese Americans who were considered as enemy aliens.

It is not the purpose of *'Holocaust' News* to assert that some Jews were not brutally treated by some Germans, that they were not uprooted and sent to live in concentration camps.

"GENOCIDE"

We do, however, assert that the allegation that more than six million Jews were deliberately exterminated in gas chambers, or otherwise, as part of a campaign of genocide is a preposterous propaganda fabrication which daily becomes more threadbare.

Further, we assert that the 'Holocaust' lie was perpetrated by Zionist-Jewry's stunning propaganda machine for the purpose of filling the minds of Gentile people the world over with such guilt feelings about the Jews that they would utter no protest when the

Above left: Although this picture, taken on April 30 by T/4 Sidney Blau, is captioned as the gas chambers being examined by a Seventh Army soldier, they are in fact the decontamination rooms for the clothing removed from the dead located at the extreme western end of the crematorium building (on the left in the photo on opposite page). *Above right:* The same door today.

The above photographs and caption are not taken from some 'neo-Nazi extremist' publication, but from issue No. 27 (1980) of the military history journal After the Battle. *It illustrates an article about Dachau by the anti-Nazi journalist and historian Andrew Mollo. We ask: Why was the room photographed originally described as a "Gas Chamber" (for killing people) and why was the door later painted over?*

'MASS GASSING' ACCOUNTS ARE SCIENTIFICALLY IMPOSSIBLE

CENTRAL to the claim that six million Jews were "systematically exterminated" by the Nazis in "death camps" is the following commonly-accepted description of how

mans – and other combatants in the war – for delousing clothing. This process is clearly described in German and French army regulations:

Firstly, the clothing was hung on racks in chambers.

seconds.

Fourthly, the chamber is then flushed with ammonia gas which reacts with the hydrogen cyanide gas to form harmless crystals.

Fifthly, indicators are used to check that the chamber is no longer

136

Zionism, aimed at the re-establishment of a Jewish national home-land, was realized with the foundation of the Jewish state of Israel in 1948. Anti-Zionism rejects the idea of Israel as a Jewish state. This is not the same as criticizing certain policies of the Israeli government. Often, individual Jews are held responsible for the actions of the Israeli government. Even violent attacks on Jewish institutions are sometimes excused in this way.

However strongly most Jews in the world feel connected with Israel, it is objectionable to translate criticism of the Israeli government into an anti-Jewish attitude. Criticism of the State of Israel is in this way used as a justification for anti-Semitism.

Zionismus ist das Streben nach einem eigenen Staat für das jüdische Volk. 1948 wurde es mit der Gründung des jüdischen Staates Israel Wirklichkeit. Der Antizionismus verwirft die Idee Israels als jüdischen Staat. Das läßt sich nicht mit Kritik an der Politik Israels gleichsetzen.

Häufig werden einzelne Juden für Maßnahmen der israelischen Regierung verantwortlich gemacht. Selbst Anschläge auf jüdische Einrichtungen werden so 'legalisiert'. Obwohl sich die meisten Juden auf der Welt mit Israel verbunden fühlen, ist es verwerflich, wenn Kritik an der israelischen Regierung zu einer anti-jüdischen Haltung führt. In diesem Fall wird Kritik an der israelischen Politik zur Rechtfertigung für Antisemitismus.

221 Antwerp, Belgium. 1982.
222 At least two men open fire in Goldenberg's, a Jewish owned restaurant in Paris. Six are killed, 22 are wounded. After the incident the owner of the restaurant, Jo Goldenberg, is about to collapse. August 9, 1982.

221 Antwerpen, 1982.
222 Am Mittag des 9. August 1982 schießen mindestens zwei Männer mit Maschinenpistolen blind auf die Gäste im jüdischen Restaurant Goldenberg in Paris. Dabei sterben 6 Menschen, 22 andere werden verletzt. Der Besitzer, Jo Goldenberg, ist nach dem Attentat dem Zusammenbruch nahe.

221

138

Who has not heard remarks like 'All Blacks are like this' or 'All Jews are like that'? From early childhood on, everyone meets certain clichés about certain groups. They are found in comics, movies, newspapers and schoolbooks, etc. When someone holds on to such negative stereotypes we speak of prejudices. Prejudices are voiced in everyday conversations, but they can also be misused for political purposes. Widely spread prejudices about 'the Jews' made it possible for the Nazis to isolate them systematically, without the opposition of many non-Jews. The same was true for gypsies and homosexuals.

Today prejudice, anti-Semitism and racism are still present in nearly every country. Examples vary from jokes and nicknames to violence and maltreatment, especially toward those groups who are identifiable and visibly different from the majority.

Combatting discrimination and racism is a matter of general interest, but not only up to the government. Specifically the individual can oppose expressions and acts of discrimination in his or her own area, school, workplace, and amongst family members and friends.

'Die Schwarzen sind so', 'die Juden sind so', wer kennt solche Äußerungen nicht? Von klein auf kommt jeder mit Bildern über bestimmte Gruppen in Kontakt. In Comics, Filmen, Zeitungen und Schulbüchern begegnet man ihnen. Wenn jemand hartnäckig an solchen Stereotypen festhält, sprechen wir von Vorurteilen. Vorurteile werden in alltäglichen Gesprächen geäußert, aber auch für politische Ziele mißbraucht. Weit verbreitete Vorurteile über 'die Juden' machten es den Nazis leicht, sie systematisch zu isolieren, ohne auf nennenswerten Widerstand zu stoßen. Dasselbe galt für Roma und Sinti oder Homosexuelle.

Auch heute begegnen wir Vorurteilen und Rassismus praktisch überall. Das drückt sich aus in Witzen und Schimpfworten bis hin zu offener Gewalt. Betroffen sind vor allem Menschen, die die Sprache nicht beherrschen oder sich äußerlich von der Mehrheit unterscheiden.

Das Eintreten gegen Rassismus und Diskriminierung ist eine Sache von allgemeinem Interesse, aber nicht allein von Staat und Regierung. Gerade der Einzelne kann diskriminierenden Äußerungen in Schule, Betrieb, Familie oder Freundeskreis begegnen.

223 *In France Le Pen's Front National receives 14,5% of the vote in the first round of the 1988 presidential elections. His main theme is: 'The French first'.*
224 *A 14-year old Asian boy, victim of racial violence in London. July 1984.*
225 *Neo-nazi's attacking Vietnamese immigrants with axes. Berlin, 1990.*

223

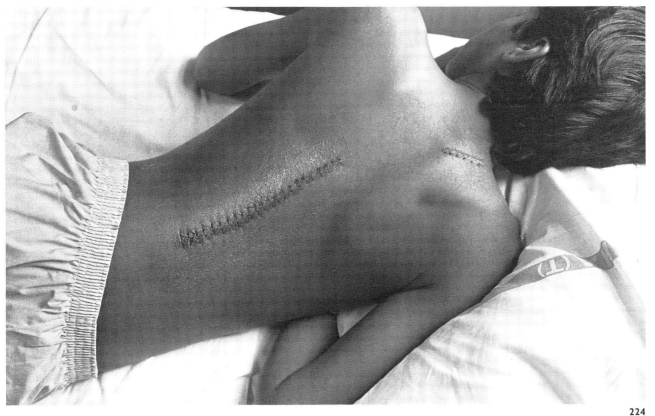

224

223 *In Frankreich erzielt die 'Front National' unter Jean-Marie Le Pen beim ersten Wahlgang der Präsidentschaftswahlen 14,5% der Stimmen. Im Mittelpunkt ihres Wahlkampfes stand die Parole: 'Erst die Franzosen.'*
224 *Ein 14 jähriger asiatischer Junge, Opfer rassistischer Gewalt. London, Juli 1984*
225 *Neonazis greifen vietnamesische Einwanderer mit Äxten an, Berlin 1990.*

225

226 International Day against Racism. This woman is carrying photographs of victims of racist violence in France. March 21, 1984.
227 Member of the extremist organisation Pamyat showing an antisemitic banner. Moscow, 1990.
228 Inhabitants of a Dutch village, Stevensbeek, clash with the police during a protest against the opening of a center for refugees in their neighborhood. October 1987.
229 S.O.S. Racisme is a French youth movement. The group is known for its concerts, festivals and demonstrations against racism and apartheid. Paris, 1985.

226 21. März 1984. Internationaler Tag gegen den Rassismus. Diese Frau trägt Fotos von Opfern rassistischer Gewalt in Frankreich bei sich.
227 Ein Mitglied der rechts-extremen Pamjat-Organisation zeigt ein antisemitisches Plakat. Moskau, 1990.
228 Als sich die Einwohner des niederländischen Dorfes Stevensbeek gegen ein Auffanglager für Flüchtlinge in ihrer Nachbarschaft wehren, kommt es zu Ausschreitungen. Oktober 1987.
229 Die Jugendorganisation SOS-Rassismus setzt sich gegen Rassismus und Apartheid ein. Sie veranstaltet große Popkonzerte, Festivals und Demonstrationen. Paris, 1985.

226

227

228

229

LIST OF ILLUSTRATIONS /
ABBILDUNGSNACHWEIS

Anne Frank Fonds, Basel/Cosmopress: 1, 2, 3, 4, 5, 6, 7, 8, 9, 10, 11, 12, 13, 108, 109, 110, 111, 112, 113, 114, 115, 116, 117, 118, 119, 120, 122, 123, 124, 125, 165, 166, 167, 168, 169, 170, 171, 172, 173, 190, 211, 212, 214.

Historisches Museum, Frankfurt am Main: 14, 15, 16, 18, 19, 21, 32, 34.

Stadtarchiv, Frankfurt am Main: 17, 36, 42, 43, 65, 72, 203.

Bundesarchiv, Koblenz: 23, 53, 54, 55, 74, 87.

Rijksinstituut voor Oorlogsdocumentatie, Amsterdam: 24, 27, 28, 29, 30, 31, 33, 35, 39, 44, 70, 71, 77, 78, 82, 85, 89, 94, 98, 99, 126, 127, 128, 129, 130, 131, 132, 133, 135, 139, 140, 143, 144, 152, 153, 157, 158, 159, 160, 161, 162, 163, 164, 174, 175, 176, 177, 178, 179, 180, 181, 191, 194, 197, 183, 184, 185, 186, 188, 189, 201, 202, 205, 208, 209, 210.

Droste Verlag, Düsseldorf: 25, 51, 52.

Staatliche Kunsthalle, Berlin: 27.

Ullstein Bilderdienst, Berlin: 33, 97, 100.

Dokumentationsarchiv des deutschen Widerstandes, Frankfurt am Main: 37, 38, 40.

Fotoarchief Spaarnestad/VNU, Haarlem: 45, 46, 47, 66, 79, 80, 81, 84, 86, 101, 102, 150, 206, 207.

Kölnisches Stadtmuseum: 48.

Yad Vashem, Jerusalem: 49, 50.

Siedler Verlag, Berlin: 75, 83.

ABC – fotoarchief, Amsterdam: 41, 76, 216, 222, 223, 226.

Privébezit: 68, 211, 212.

Gemeentearchief Amsterdam: 104, 105, 106, 107, 137, 138, 151, 182.

Gemeentearchief Den Haag: 134, 146, 148, 192, 193.

Gemeentearchief Rotterdam: 136, 153, 199.

Bildarchiv Preussischer Kulturbesitz, Berlin: 67.

Bildarchiv Pisarek, Berlin: 90, 91, 92, 93.

Joods Historisch Museum, Amsterdam: 156.
ANP: 228.

RBP/GAMMA: 218, 227, 229.

Steef Meijknecht: 215.

John Melskens: 213.

David Hoffmann: 224.

Cas Oorthuys: 158, 195.

Amsterdams Historisch Museum: 141.

Charles Breijer: 145, 155, 198.

Ad Windig: 196, 200.

Stichting Lau Mazirel, Amsterdam: 187.

Stadtarchiv Hadamar: 59.

Archiv Ernst Klee: 60.

Stadtarchiv Waldshut-Tiegen: 96

A. Nussbaum: 154

J. Escher: 187

Sacha/Transworld: 225.

COLOPHON

144

This book was produced on the occasion of the exhibition
'Anne Frank in the World, 1929-1945'.
Photo research and text: Dienke Hondius, Joke Kniesmeijer and
Bauco T. van der Wal.
Photo research in Frankfurt: Jürgen Steen, Historisch Museum,
Frankfurt.
Coordination of translations and production: Jan Erik Dubbelman.
Didactical interpretation: Cor Suijk.
English language text provided by: Steven Arthur Cohen,
Dewar MacLeod.
Printed by Veenman, Wageningen
Cover design: Marius van Leeuwen, Amsterdam.
Graphic design and lay-out: Marius van Leeuwen and Nel Punt,
Amsterdam.
Lithograph: AB-Graphics Amsterdam and Veenman, Wageningen
Typeset by Agema Photosetting, Amsterdam.

IMPRESSUM

Buch zur Ausstellung 'Die Welt der Anne Frank 1929-1945'
Bildredaktion und Text: Dienke Hondius, Joke Kniesmeijer,
Bauco T. van der Wal
Recherchen über Frankfurt: Dr. Jürgen Steen, Historisches
Museum, Frankfurt
Koordination von Übersetzungen und Produktion:
Jan Erik Dubbelman
Englische Übersetzung: Steven Arthur Cohen, Dewar MacLeod
Deutsche Übersetzung: Martin Randt, Alex Suijk
Umschlagentwurf: Marius van Leeuwen
Lay-out: Marius van Leeuwen, Nel Punt, Amsterdam
Satz: Agema Photosetting, Amsterdam
Druck: Veenman, Wageningen
Lithographie: AB-GRAPHIC und Projectiecolor, Hoofddorp